D0264732

MYSTERIOUS SCOTLAND

Tangled threid and rowan seed
Gar the witches lowse their speed.

Mendelssohn first visited the cave on Staffa on 8 August 1829; the first bars (above) of his Hebridean Overture (or Fingal's Cave) are said to have been written in the vast cave, surrounded by huge basalt pillars like organ pipes.

Mysterious SCOTLAND

MICHAEL BALFOUR

MAINSTREAM
PUBLISHING
EDINBURGH AND LONDON

For Elisabeth

with love and thanks

424879

941 BAL

GL

Copyright © Michael Balfour, 1997

All rights reserved

The moral right of the author has been asserted

First published in Great Britain in 1997 by
MAINSTREAM PUBLISHING COMPANY (EDINBURGH) LTD
7 Albany Street
Edinburgh EH1 3UG

ISBN 1 85158 695 4

No part of this book may be reproduced or transmitted in any form or by any other means without permission in writing from the publisher, except by a reviewer who wishes to quote brief passages in connection with a review written for insertion in a magazine, newspaper or broadcast

'The Loch Ness Monster's Song' on p8 is reproduced with kind permission of Carcanet Press Ltd

A catalogue record for this book is available from the British Library

All photographs © Michael Balfour 1997, except those credited otherwise

Designed by Jenny Haig

Typeset in Centaur
Printed by H & Y Printing Ltd, Hong Kong

CONTENTS

The saltire in a very strange place — by the A939 between Grantown-on-Spey and Tomintoul.

ACKNOWLEDGEMENTS

No book of this nature could possibly have been researched and written, and all the photographs taken, without the assistance of a great number of people. First and foremost I would like to thank the Scottish Tourist Board in Edinburgh, together with the individual offices of the area Tourist Board network, for their detailed and efficient attention to my needs for a book which covers such a wide range of subjects. I was the Board's overnight guest at a great number of fine and recommended establishments all over Scotland, and to those I give my thanks again for their universally warm welcome and generous hospitality. The savings involved were crucial to my enterprise.

Caledonian MacBrayne were extremely helpful with my ambitious travel plans, and gladly sailed me about in comfortable and punctual ferries on their near-legendary inter-island routes. P & O Ferries were also kind in carrying me to the Orkney Islands and back. All the while I was dictating many thousands of words of notes into a pocket recorder afforded me by Philips. Its handy portability in gale-force winds proved its worth on many occasions.

I am grateful to Carcanet Press for allowing me to quote 'The Loch Ness Monster's Song' by Edwin Morgan (1990), and to Orkney Press for the use of a few lines from 'The Symbol Stones of Scotland' (1984) by Anthony Jackson. Thanks also to Geoffrey Bles for permission to quote from *The Arches of the Years* by Halliday Sutherland.

My conversations with Lady Cawdor, John MacLeod of MacLeod and the Marquis of Northampton added unexpected dimensions to my accounts of their castle dwellings. In so many of these great homes I was received with much kindness by their owners. Donald Little gave me hours of his time at Fyvie Castle, where he is curator. And so on, at prehistoric and historic sites and buildings all over Scotland which are simply too numerous to mention.

I thank Bill Campbell at Mainstream Publishing for the opportunity to write and illustrate *Mysterious Scotland*, Jenny Haig for this handsome design, and Cathy Mineards for being a caring and wise editor. Love's labours were not lost.

Amanda Howard has again, with skill, good humour and constant efficiency, typed another book from my dripping quill. And Susan Vaughan has again made me a thorough index which we trust will prove of immense help to readers (see author's note below).

Finally, my heartfelt thanks to Elisabeth Ingles, who travelled with me to most ends of Scotland, as well as the bits in between. We shan't forget a late-night 'takeaway haggis' in Thurso. With the blood of her Scottish forebears, a degree from Edinburgh University and a knowledge of '1745 and All That' imbibed from childhood, she supported and fortified me in endless ways.

Author's note: Regional locations of place-names will be found in the index

The Loch Ness Monster's Song

By Edwin Morgan

Sssnnnwhufffffll?
Hnwhuffl hhnnwfl hnfl hfl?
Gdroblboblhobngbl gbl gl g g g g glbgl.
Drublhaflablhaflubhafgabhafhafl fl fl —
gm grawwwww grf grawf awfgm graw gm.
Hovoplodok-doplodovok-plovodokot-doplodokosh?
Splgraw fok fok splgrafhatchgabrlgabrl fok splfok!
Zgra kra gka fok!
Grof grawff gahf?
Gombl mbl bl —
blm plm,
blm plm,
blm plm,
blp.

Edwin Morgan says that this is a lonely monster's swearing session, after he failed to find the reptile companions of his youth in the depths of the Loch. It first appeared in his collection *From Glasgow to Saturn* (1973), and is in his *Collected Poems* (Carcanet Press, 1990). Edwin Morgan was born in 1920 and educated at Glasgow University, where he is now Titular Professor of Poetry.

INTRODUCTION

I returned from my long journeys around Scotland for this book convinced of one great fact: that it really is a nation unto itself. It has its own Church, cuisine, currency, education system, folklore, language (in the Western Isles), laws, music, painting schools, politics and sports. And it possesses an incomparable range of mysteries, the likes of which would have been long forgotten elsewhere. These 11 chapters bring you a necessarily eclectic selection of these. I have searched far and wide on the ground, and high and low in libraries, for early sources of tales from long ago. I have endeavoured to exclude many stories which constantly reappear, and to bring in the odd, the quirky, and the unanswerable, of the 'we may never know' variety. Questions are so often more interesting than answers.

Scottish nationalists have been feeling bruised for a very long time. They should take heart from a recent one of their number, the Old Etonian Eric Arthur Blair (1903–1950), otherwise known as George Orwell. Two years after he finished writing *Animal Farm* in his house on Jura, he reminded the nationalists that 'after all, the Communist Manifesto was once a very obscure document, and the Nazi Party only had six members when Hitler joined it'.

Nationalists have always been very uncomfortable with what is the biggest Scottish mystery — and it didn't take place in Scotland — summarised in eight words: 'Why did Bonnie Prince Charlie stop at Derby?'

The story goes like this. In early December 1745 London panicked. Prince Charles Edward Stuart was leading his army south of the border, and heading for Derby where people were in a panic, shops boarded up, State Lottery sales diminished, playhouse performances cancelled, pamphleteers scaring citizens out of their wits with lively descriptions of Highlanders and their habits, religious zealots warning of Catholic ways, anti-riot soldiers spreading out through the capital . . . and troops assembling to march north. The Bank of England feared a run on its reserves and paid out depositors in sixpences only — heated on stoves so they were difficult to remove. Too hot to handle.

On 6 December 1745 Derby fell to the Prince . . . and he then decided to go no further. To all Jacobites that day became known as Black Friday. Had he continued his march south he would, it seemed then and it seems now, have taken London and all England. Nearly two hundred years later, George V (1865–1936) confirmed once again the lingering presence of Scotland's greatest mystery beyond its borders in a chat with the Duke of Atholl: 'Had Charles Edward gone on from Derby I should not have been King of England today.'

I am confident that there are strange objects stored away in Scotland's thousand and more castles which will never be seen. One which can is in the West Highland Museum in Fort William. *The Secret Portrait* is an anamorphic painting, a deliberately contrived distortion that can be seen correctly only when viewed at a certain angle. The technique of controlling perspective was known in the fifteenth century and used by Leonardo da Vinci. In this case, the distortion is reflected in a shining metal cylinder, a method introduced to the West from China.

Prince Charles Edward, Bonnie Prince Charlie, was an obvious subject for an anamorphic portrait because after the 1745 rising and his subsequent defeat at Culloden it was treasonable to support the Stuart claim to the throne. After the ladies and servants left the room at the end of a dinner, loyal friends of Prince Charles would place the tray in the centre of the table, and then raise their glasses in a toast to the likeness by now reflected in the cylinder. If there was a danger of interruption or discovery, the cylinder was quickly removed and the painted tray then appeared as a meaningless blur. The artist is unknown and there is no record of the portrait's owners. It was discovered by chance in a London shop by the founder of the museum and is one of its most fascinating exhibits. The whole point of its use is of course that *The Secret Portrait* can only be seen while standing up, as the Prince's supporters naturally would have been when drinking the loyal toast.

A century later, Scottish perceptions of London-based royalty had changed. The visit of Queen Victoria and Prince Albert in the summer of 1842 was one of the first few royal visits since the coronation of Charles II in 1651, and it was an event of great excitement. *The Perthshire Advertiser and Strathmore Journal* carried an article

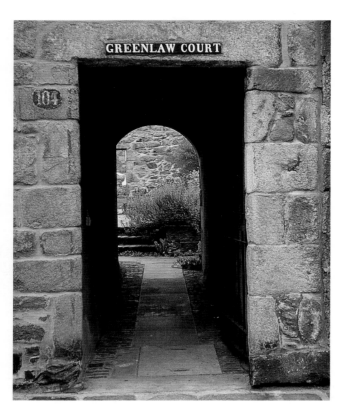

The doorway to Greenlaw Court is just to the south of the cross in the High Street of old Aberdeen. 'Green', 'Law' and 'Court' are constituent parts of very ancient place-names and, found together, indicate prehistoric law-making.

on 18 August 1842 which read, in part, as follows:

> Our readers will share the delight that we experience in learning of Her Majesty's intention to visit Scotland towards the end of the present month.
>
> The people of Scotland are pre-eminently distinguished by a reverent regard for constituted authority, and we are quite assured that the first Magistrate of the Empire would receive from them a loyal and cordial welcome out of respect for the offices even though the character of the monarch did not present any particular claims to their esteem. But Queen Victoria is happily the possessor of virtues which give additional lustre to her station, and challenge the warmest love and veneration of her subjects . . .
>
> The senseless pageantry by which it was sought to honour the visit of George IV to Scotland would be particularly out of place in the present circumstances of the country; and the sudden and unostentatious manner in which the Queen's purpose has been made is another proof of her consideration and judgement and it shows that it is her wish that her progress through Scotland should be attended by as little pomp

and circumstance as possible and with no unnecessary inconvenience to the people.

> The Queen's first visit to the land of 'brown heather and shaggy wood' must indeed be marked by some demonstration worthy of and suitable to the occasion, but we trust that it will be of a character more becoming to the intelligence of the nation than the costly and ridiculous fooleries which signalised the visit of her uncle.

The word 'fooleries' was in reference to the activities of Queen Victoria's uncle, King George IV (1762–1830), who made a private visit to Edinburgh in 1822. He concentrated his energies the whole time upon his appetites for food, money and women – and not necessarily in that order.

In 1853 the Balmoral estate was purchased by the royal family and they occupied it for the first time, after considerable rebuilding, three years later, Queen Victoria at last achieving her long-held dream of having her own estate in the Highlands. She was certainly constitutionally up to a draughty existence. She records on one page of her diary: 'We had travelled 69 miles today and 60 yesterday . . . Did not feel tired. We ladies did not dress, and dined *en famille*, looking at maps of the Highlands after dinner.' Those miles were travelled partly on horseback and partly by carriage, on rough, stony trackways.

Queen Victoria wrote to a great friend of hers of her faith in John Brown, a local man and her hand-servant: 'He is an excellent, handy servant, able to do anything . . . He is also an invaluable, shrewd and trustworthy man.' In February 1865 she wrote in her diary: 'Have decided that Brown should remain permanently and make himself useful in other ways beside leading my pony, as he is so very dependable.'

Mysteries, in this land so well stocked with them, continue to arise. Scotland is the only country in the world to have commemorated an encounter with a UFO. The monument was erected in January 1992 on Dechmont Law, West Lothian, by the Livingston Development Corporation, the then employers of Bob Taylor, a forester. Soon after ten o'clock in the morning on 9 November 1989, Taylor found proof of Cicero's adage: 'Walk where we will, we walk upon some story.'

He was in Dechmont Forest and came to a clearing he knew well. But he didn't know anything at all about what was standing there – and neither would anybody else in the world have done. He was looking up at a 25-

foot-high round 'object' with a rim around its middle — just like flying saucer pictures in comics. Then it changed colour, becoming almost transparent, and two spherical 'figures' with lots of outstretched limbs rolled out towards him and grabbed him by the trouser legs. Then Bob Taylor fainted, with the smell of burning all around him. The local police were later taken by him, trousers all singed, to the clearing, and they found no 'object' but giant twin tracks and about 30 holes in the ground. They were angled outwards. The legs of a giant pod may well have stood in them.

The commemorative plaque is not, however, to be found in that clearing in the forest. Arthur C. Clarke, in his book *Mysterious Worlds*, located the incident on Dechmont Law, and so the Livingston Development Corporation decided that the commemorative plaque should be set there upon a rock.

B ut the most important physical feature of the country is water. It is the weather in Scotland which accounts for the *severitas* in the Scottish character, particularly north of the Central Lowlands where only about 25 per cent of the population dwells. It was the co-founder of the *Edinburgh Review* (in 1802), Sydney Smith (1771–1845), who shrewdly observed that 'no nation has so large a stock of benevolence of heart as the Scotch. Their temper stands anything but an attack on their climate'.

One watery legend, immortalised in an opera, originally had a Scottish setting. Richard Wagner's *The Flying Dutchman* (1843) was never going to be called *The Flying Scotsman*, but it was a close call. His heroine's father, Daland, was to have been called Donald, while her slightly drippy boyfriend Erik would have been called Georg (in the German form). Wagner's plot was based on Heinrich Heine's version of the legend, with its Scottish background. Unfortunately, a little-known French composer, one Pierre-Louis Dietsch, had the same idea, and his opera was first performed two months before Wagner's was due. Dietsch's libretto was not pinched from Wagner; he put it together from many sources, including the works of Sir Walter Scott and Captain Frederick Marryat, but the result also had a Scottish setting, and Wagner was therefore forced to make changes at the last minute. The rival opera, *Le Vaisseau Fantôme*, sank without trace.

Scotland, all of which is west of the prime meridian at Greenwich, covers 29,796 square miles, over a third of the British Isles. North of the meandering 100-mile border with England lie 631 square miles of inland

One of the Mortality Stones inside the Cathedral church of St Andrews in Dornoch. The Cathedral was built between 1224 and 1239 by St Gilbert of Moray (died 1245), the last Scotsman to be canonised before the Reformation.

water: the lochs, which have been the scenes of so much drama. Around them stretch 5,556.24 miles of coastline, of which a stretch about 0.24 miles long in Argyll is a mere 12 miles from Ireland, whence Scotland's founders sailed.

Water irrigates daily life in Scotland. Down the centuries its history has also been moistened more than a little by blood. The shedding of it, in causes both common and otherwise, fills the history books to which this book is no more than an addendum. I have had to omit, for example, the tales of derring-do around Loch Lomond, Stirling and the Trossachs of 'Rob Roy' (Gaelic for Red Robert) MacGregor (1671–1734), and his unusually long arms. He rests now in the historic kirkyard of Balquhidder at the east end of Loch Voil in Perthshire — MacGregor country. His sporran is on view at Inveraray Castle.

I make little mention of the early history of the Lords of the Isles, preferring not to disturb the guide books and brochures and their reflections of Sir Walter Scott's lofty tamperings. Their original name was *Ri Innse Gall*, which means 'Kings of the Isles'. The Western Isles were ruled from the Isle of Man on behalf of the Norsemen until Somerled (died 1164)

The recumbent stone in Midmar Kirkyard, resting between its two extra-tall flanking stones.

This map of Mull, which hangs in the Mishnish Hotel in Tobermory, suggests that the island is a kind of squashed Britain.

The Secret Portrait of Bonnie Prince Charlie, in the West Highland Museum in Fort William (Photograph: R. Matassa).

took them in 1156–58. This progenitor of the clan Donald established a council of 14 barons, based on a castle (now in ruins) in Islay, on Loch Finlagan, south-west of Port Askaig. His son Reginald promulgated the first laws of Gaeldom, and the barons sat in council and judgement on the island of Comhairle in the loch. James IV ended the dynasty in 1493.

Nor have I gone much into the fact that there is a long-established body of believers in the genealogy of 64 directly succeeding generations between Tephi, the daughter of Zedekiah, the last king of Judah and Jerusalem (from 597 BC), and Kenneth mac Alpin, king of the 'Scots' of Dalriada, who also became king of the Picts *c*.843 when Alba (to become Scotland) was formed. The bottom line in this theory is that Queen Elizabeth II is descended from the Royal House of Zarah-Judath through the Davidic line as well as through the Levitical Aaronic line.

R obert Burns normally looms large in indexes at the end of books on Scotland, and quite right too. He is of course present in *Mysterious Scotland* – and here is an early taste of the incorrigible character of the Ayrshire Poet. He once found himself in an old inn in the village of Inver, at the mouth of the Dornoch Firth. He was chatting to the landlord when the landlord's very obstreperous wife appeared on the scene. The landlord

was thoroughly fed up with her and handed her into the care of the poet, which was possibly not a very wise move. After dallying with her awhile he was rid of her, and reached for the diamond he always carried in his pocket. He scratched these lines dedicated to the landlord on a window in his inn:

> Ye gods, ye gave to me a wife out o' your grace and
>   pleasure,
> To be the partner of my life, and I was glad to have her;
> If your Providence Divine for better things design her,
> T'obey your will, at any time, I am willing to resign her.

The Black Bull hotel in Moffat was established in 1568. John Graham of Claverhouse (1648–1689), after serving in French and Dutch armies, held the King's commission to suppress the Covenanters in the south-west in 1683–85. He made the hotel his headquarters, ruthlessly achieved his ends, and got called Bluidy Claverhouse. When Robert Burns stayed in the hotel he heard again this terrible tale, which induced in him a fit of remorse for his own previous bad behaviour. He reached once more into his pocket for his diamond, and scratched on a window:

> Ask why God made the gem so small and why so huge
>   the granite,
> Because God meant tha' man should set the higher
>   value on it.

Cup and ring marks on one of the stones at Balnuaran of Clava. They are found throughout the world but nobody has discovered their meaning.

The island of Lismore at dusk, viewed from Oban (which Virginia Woolf called 'the Ramsgate of the North').

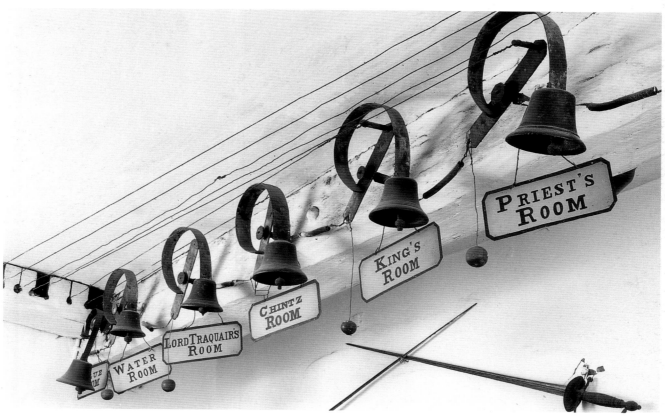

Bells in the servants' quarters at Traquair House (photograph from the owner).

The Star Hotel in Moffat. It is Scotland's narrowest, and is just 20 feet one inch wide.

I stayed in Moffat during my travels, at the Star Hotel, which is the narrowest in Britain at 20 feet and one inch. The manufacturer's name on the toilet roll dispensers there is SelfServe Hygiene Ltd. I am not sure what should have boggled. I suspected at the time that it should have been my imagination.

If you like the sound of your voice you should try shouting on the island of Ailsa Craig, in 'lonely sublimity', as William Wordsworth put it, in the Clyde Estuary. You get many seconds of repetition there. It has long been called Fairy Rock, but its more popular nickname these days is Paddy's Milestone, because Glasgow's Irish inhabitants reckon that the island is half-way to Belfast.

The longest echo possible inside a building in Scotland is unquestionably in the Hamilton Mausoleum, between East Kilbride and Motherwell. A vast palace was built south of it by the tenth Duke of Hamilton (1767–1852), but this had to be demolished in the 1920s because of subsidence into the coal mines below. The mausoleum was designed for him by the greatest Scottish architect in the baronial style, Edinburgh-born David Bryce (1803–1876). There are eight empty alcoves in the octagonal chapel; sing into one and your voice will echo all around you like an unearthly choir for about 25 seconds. This is why the chapel can never be used.

David Bryce also designed the British Linen Bank (1846–1851) in Edinburgh, which now houses the Bank of Scotland. Scotsmen have always been good bankers. The national parsimony inspired this observation by Edwin Muir in his book *Scottish Journey* (1935): 'I think it is possible that all Scots are illegitimate, Scotsmen being so mean and Scotswomen so generous.'

Both the Bank of England (1694) and the Bank of Scotland (1696) were founded by a Scottish financier, William Paterson (1658–1719), who was born in the most humble circumstances on a remote Dumfriesshire farm. In 1826 the House of Commons threatened to enact a Bill withdrawing the Bank of Scotland's right to issue its own banknotes. Sir Walter Scott led a successful campaign to have the Bill dropped, but using the pseudonym Malachi Malagrowther. I suspect this is an anagram . . . ideas to me, please, care of Mainstream Publishing!

There are some deliciously perverse aspects in the Scottish profile. It has long been held, for example, that the purest English is spoken on the Black Isle, which is not black, an island, or in England.

An old April Fools' Day joke is played in the Orkney Islands. On Tailing Day tails or rude messages are pinned on people's backs, in honour of the Celtic god Lud, god of humour among much else. But this all takes place on 2 April and not 1 April, which the rest of us use for foolery. But still, these are the islands where, early in the eighteenth century, a woman in Stromness made her living selling winds to mariners. They were priced at a pretty steep sixpence each.

In 1831 Aeneas Coffey invented a continuous distilling process which made possible the manufacture of whisky in bulk; he was an Irishman. Tartans and bagpipes originated outside Scotland – a kingdom of which Idi Amin once had himself crowned King . . .

This is the country where you still hear of St Fillan, the seventh-century missionary who used a cave in Cove Wynd at Pittenweem, in East Neuk, Fife, as a place of worship. Inside it there is a well and also an altar where he used to write, with the aid of a luminous glow from his left arm.

In the Highlands and islands you can enjoy the euphonious beauty of the Gaelic language and the meaning of words; here are four place names: *Achnashellach*, field of the willows; *Ardnamurchan*, point of the ocean; *Ballachulish*, township of the narrows; *Inchnadamph*, meadow of the stag.

This is the country that typically acquired its national emblem in battle. In 990, on the eve of the Battle of Luncarty, near Perth, invading Danes were creeping up on Kenneth II's sleeping forces. To avoid making any noise they walked barefoot – into a field of thistles, cried out in pain, and were routed.

A distant forebear was christened Robert Lewis Balfour Stevenson (1850–1894). He later dropped his mother's maiden name, and at 18 preferred Louis, because he and all his family loathed a town councillor called Lewis. He had this to say about the 'duties' I have so much enjoyed in researching and writing *Mysterious Scotland*; and I hope I have represented him well: 'There are two distinct duties incumbent on any man who enters on the business of writing: truth to the fact and a good spirit in the treatment.'

☆ ★ ☆ ★ ☆ ★ ☆

Michael Balfour

Chapter One

THE OLD STONES

Only 5,000 years before the stones at Callanish were erected on the island the nearby Butt of Lewis was an utterly remote north-westerly point on the continent of Europe. The English Channel did not then exist and there were many fewer Scottish islands. Eleven thousand years ago you could, as it were, have walked along the roof of the Channel Tunnel to France.

The dawn of Scotland's prehistory revealed landscapes, mountain ranges, rivers, lochs and forests, of which many remain today. It is the primeval feelings that parts of Scotland evoke in us that are so appealing. All over the country, not just in the Highlands and the northern and western islands, it is possible to stand in a place where no man has ever stood before, and contemplate a view which does not feature a single man-made object. The purity and solitude of the experience is not to be had almost anywhere else in the British Isles, and you learn that silence has its own noise.

Natural geography creates history in due course. Because nowhere in Scotland is more than 40 miles from salt water, it was along the rivers, around the lochs, over the passes, through the glens, and to good new pastures that prehistoric northern man migrated. At the time of the rising North Sea levels about 11,000 years ago, as the ice of that age retreated north, the lower lying lands of Scotland were all forest. Travel was in wooden dug-out and coracle-type boats. Then came sledges and afterwards wheeled transport, about the eighth century BC. The first hunters and food gatherers went into the forests for roe deer, red deer (then much larger than now), boar and wild cattle (now extinct). Good land was cleared; fires provided food preparation and warmth. Stone and flint, and then bronze and iron, steadily acquired remarkably skilled users.

The great auk of 11,000 years ago is gone for ever, but above the wolves and bears in the undergrowth there flew grouse we would recognise, and blackcock and capercailzie. They too were snared and hung over the fires, and later cooked with berry juices and herbs in pots, from about 5,000 years ago. The decoration and styles of such pots are quite as useful as hallmarks on fine metals for dating, provenance and the tracking of migratory movements. Neolithic pottery from southern England has been found on Tiree.

Scotland before Christ, in prehistory, has only its archaeology to provide us with a profile of evolving those skills. History from prehistory derives from radiocarbon and thermoluminescence dating techniques for artefacts and the first buildings. Examples of the everyday hardware of the first people to inhabit Scotland – we cannot call them Scotsmen – are all around us, and they are made of stone.

The old stones of Scotland, as dressed and erected by Neolithic man, include among their number a group of circles in the Gordon district, west of Aberdeen, the likes of which are not found anywhere else in the world (except, that is, for a small number in south-west Ireland, which raises obvious questions and adds to their puzzle). They are known as recumbent stone circles, because their upright pillars are interrupted, always in the south-west quadrants, by huge oblong stones lying on the ground. These recumbent stones are, in every case, closely flanked by extra-tall upright stones (but only in comparison with their immediate neighbours).

Seventy-four of these circles or rings (most are elliptical) occur in the area, and almost all of them are located on sloping ground and have extensive open views. They average 12 stones, including the one lying down, with the tallest stones always placed on the lower side. The recumbent stones are always the largest, up to 20 feet long and weighing up to 50 tons. And it is an odd fact that their inner sides are all placed about 18 inches inside the ring. Nobody knows why.

The Gaelic for 'Are you going to church?' is *Am bheil thu dol d'on chlachan?* This question translates literally as 'Are you going to the stones?'. The old idea dies hard that churches on raised circular sites are where rings of stone once stood. Midmar is about 15 miles west of Aberdeen, beyond Echt. In 1914 a graveyard was established around the recent church there, and *also* around a 57-foot diameter recumbent stone circle which is more than 4,000 years old. A local lady, who says she is called 'The White Witch', has told me that her Irish Setter, 'Bracken', has never ventured inside the circle.

It has been agreed that these unique structures were not erected for sepulchral purposes, and neither were they burial cairns. Indeed, neither were Stonehenge, Avebury and most others among Britain's 900 or so stone circles intended to hold central burials. It cannot be argued that they are ruins of brochs, those strange round, drystone, fortified homesteads of which about 500 remain, mostly in the west and Highlands. The recumbent stones, sometimes called ghost doors, were never lintels either. Sixteen of them bear cupmarks, but only ever on the recumbent stones or their flankers.

The recumbent stone circle called Loanhead of Daviot, near Inverurie, north-west of Aberdeen, is a splendid example – and it falls exactly on an invisible straight line with New Craig stone circle (and is visible from it) and the site of a now-destroyed stone circle in the kirkyard at Daviot. A few years ago the Scottish surveyor Professor Alexander Thom proved that the distance from the circle's exact centre to the edge of its inner cairn is precisely 20 megalithic yards. Each of these represents 2.72 feet and appears to be the common unit of measurement employed by prehistoric man. The distance from the cairn edge to the inner circle edge is a further five megalithic yards. The 'outlier' stones, beyond the circle to the south-east, make it probable that the whole edifice was an instrument of prediction for midwinter sunrises.

Conflicting theories about the origins and purposes of these recumbent stone circles have all flourished through the ages. Hector Boece (or Boethius;

I am told that there are people who do not care for maps, and find it hard to believe. The names, the shapes of the woodlands, the courses of the roads and rivers, the prehistoric footsteps of man still distinctly traceable up hill and down dale, the mills and the ruins, the ponds and the ferries, perhaps the Standing Stone or the Druidic Circle on the heath; here is an inexhaustible fund of interest for any man with eyes to see, or tuppence worth of imagination to understand with.

— from *A Note Concerning Treasure Island*
by Robert Louis Stevenson

c.1465–1536) studied philosophy in Paris, and became friends with Erasmus. Later he became the first principal of Aberdeen University, which he helped to found. The fact that at the same time he was also canon of Aberdeen Cathedral makes this renowned Scottish historian's comments on these unique local stone circles, in his 1527 *Chronicles*, most challenging:

To promote religion amongst his people King Mainus . . . instituted new and customary ceremonies in honour of the gods, over and above the older ritual. In various localities of his territories, according as the circumstances required, huge stones were assembled in a ring, and the biggest of them was stretched out on the south side (of the ring) to serve for an altar, whereon were burnt the victims in sacrifice to the gods. In proof of the fact to this day there stand these mighty stones gathered into circles . . . 'the old temples of the gods' they are commonly called — and whoso sees them will assuredly marvel by what mechanical craft or by what bodily strength stones of such bulk have been collected to one spot. The 'victim' of those days was that portion of grain or of cattle which was by heathen custom due to the gods, or so much of it as was not required for the maintenance of the priests, who were in those times very few.

Boece's mention of the giant recumbent stones as altar stones supports the idea that the flat dais stone slabs, let into the ground just inside the horizontal stones, were where the astronomer-priests stood — and not for burying the dead, but rather for addressing the living within the circles. In the centre, 'need fires' would be lit in May and November, as confirmed by finds of burnt earth, bone scraps and early Beaker

One of the rings of stone at Loanhead of Daviot.

A tranquil scene at Balnuaran of Clava, where the cairn rubble is tightly ringed, not far from the field of Culloden.

pottery sherds. And it also seems that law has long been involved with Scotland's old stones.

It is recorded that on 2 May 1349 a court was held at Candle Hill of Old Rayne at Insch, north-west of Aberdeen, attended by the King's justiciar. In 1380 a Court of Regality took place 'apud le stand and stanes de la Rath de Kingusie' at the Hill of Fiddes, Garioch, attended by Alexander, son of Robert II. It was to investigate the Bishop of Moray's title to certain lands, and the Bishop was required to stand *extra circum* — outside the circle.

Sir Walter Scott thought of the circles as Viking temples or Odin and Norse courts of justice, but they are definitely pre-Viking. It is true though that the *tings* (stone circles) in the Orkney Isles were used as courts as late as 1602. In the eighteenth century such circles were referred to as Temple Stars and Law Stones. Until the 1860s, oaths taken with hands joined through the hole in the (now vanished) Woden's Stone at Stenness, on Mainland in the Orkneys, were considered solemn and binding by the courts of law.

Some puzzling facts about the recumbent stone circles will probably always remain so. For example, why are the lone horizontal stones so often of a different geological material from the other stones in the ring? They are at Garrol Wood, Hatton of Ardoyne, Sunhoney (200 yards north-west of the farm), Raes of Clune and Old Keig, all west of Aberdeen. At the last site the recumbent stone of sillimanite gneiss weighs about 53 tons, and it was dragged all the way from Don Valley, no less than six miles away. Why is one, and only ever one, of the two upright flanking stones always slightly out of line? And what of the cupmarks found carved on 16 of these Neolithic sites — but only ever on the horizontal stones or their flankers? Rothiemay, five miles north of Huntly, has 119 of them . . . events records, invocations, maps of the constellations? Mysteries there will always be around Aberdeen.

The word 'pagan' stems from the Latin *paganus*, meaning 'civilian', as opposed to *miles*, 'soldier', and grew to mean 'heathen', i.e. not Christian or Jewish. This differential has gone on to give 'pagan practices' a bad press, but I wonder whether this is fair, given the survival of so many of them from prehistoric times into our own.

It was a Scotsman who invented the word 'prehistoric'. Daniel Wilson (1816–1892) used it in his book *The Archaeology and Prehistoric Annals of Scotland* (1851), to replace the too literal 'antehistoria'.

Early Christians generally took care to take over 'pagan sites of worship', and so many festivals and saint's day practices survive in Scotland. If you see a round and raised up kirkyard, just imagine the ring of stones which probably once stood there. Often you will find unusually large pieces of stone in the church fabric at ground level, or perhaps used as a lintel above the porch, or, more often, over the church door itself. If the kirkyard is walled, check it for very large stones.

The Roman emperor Theodosius I (the Great, a Spaniard) ordered pagan shrines to be dedicated to Christian churches in 392. His second son, Honorius, issued an order in 408 forbidding the destruction of 'heathen temples' in areas of dense population.

In 601 Pope Gregory I consigned Abbot Mellitus to Britain. He was to become Archbishop of Canterbury in 619, died there in 624 and was later canonised. The Pope (Gregory the Great, a doctor and the first monk to be elected Pope) gave him a letter of instruction to take with him for Bishop Augustine. It included this passage:

> When (by God's help) you come to our most reverend brother, Bishop Augustine, I want you to tell him how earnestly I have been pondering over the affairs of the English: I have come to the conclusion that the temples of the idols in England should not on any account be destroyed. Augustine must smash the idols, but the temples themselves should be sprinkled with holy water and altars set up in them in which relics are to be enclosed. For we ought to take advantage of well-built temples by purifying them from devil-worship and dedicating them to the service of the true God. In this way, I hope the people (seeing their temples are not destroyed) will leave their idolatry and yet continue to frequent the places as formerly, so coming to know and revere the true God.

Those words are one reason for the survival of a standing stone (or menhir) called 'St Marnan's Chair' in the kirkyard of Marnoch Church, midway between Keith and Turriff in Banff and Buchan. It is over eight feet high above the ground, and could possibly have been next to a recumbent stone.

☆ ★ ☆ ★ ☆ ★ ☆

Pictish stones and some place names, such as Pitlochry (there are about 320 'Pit-' place names in Scotland, most frequently in Aberdeen, Fife, ~~Kinross~~ Angus and Perth) are all that remain of one of the great Scottish mysteries: the Picts. First mentioned by Eumenius, the Roman orator and teacher, in 297,

The ruins of Arbroath Abbey (right), the refectory, and the bishop's lodgings (left).

A lonely yet once-important stone circle near the village of Kinnell.

A chambered cairn at Balnuaran of Clava.

where did they come from, and why did they vanish so suddenly after 843, when they were united with the Scots under Kenneth mac Alpin? Hundreds of their symbol stones can be seen all over Scotland, in both remote landscapes and familiar places, such as the castles of Glamis, Braemar and Balmoral. Why are they never far from water? Knowledge of their original purposes is lost – or is it entirely? Their symbols are, it seems, limited to only 28; they are divided into four groups of seven, and are always carved on the stones in pairs.

Picts were first so-called by the Romans; *Pictus* is Latin for 'painted' under Galgacus (the first known 'Scottish' name). But Hadrian's Wall had to be built to confine these fine and wild people, starting in 120, and the Antonine Wall in 143. The Romans finally quit in 410.

The largest Pictish sculptured stone (now housed in an ultra-modern glass case) is Sueno's Stone ('Sven's Stone') near Forres, on the way to Findhorn. It is a 20 foot-high sandstone slab, with a huge wheelcross on one side and nearly 100 figures carved on the other. It could be a commemorative funerary monument, sited as it is on the border of the old Pictish kingdom of

Moray, and was probably carved at the end of the last of the three classes of Pictish stones (*c.*790–842). Fine Pictish symbol stones are also to be seen in the Gordon district at Brandsbutt, Inverurie, in Kintore Kirkyard, and in Rhynie, to the west, both in the square and in the kirkyard.

It is not known why Picts only inherited through the female line (the matrilinear system), and intermarried in groups of four lineages – a practice found in ancient creation myths.

And so the great Dark Age mystery: the symbol stones and a few place names, but nothing else of the fierce Picts, their language, culture, artefacts, settlements, or even their burial customs. Unlike their prehistoric predecessors, they evidently did not use stone for their tombs but only, in fact, for message boards about land holdings.

Mysterious though the Pictish symbol stones may be, cup and cup and ring marks also ultimately remain a complete enigma throughout every country in Europe. These Neolithic and Bronze Age petroglyphs were most often carved on stone outcrops (extremely rarely on free-standing boulders), at unfortified sites with open views, generally to the south, towards water,

The Trushal Stone on the Isle of Lewis in the Western Isles, one of the tallest in Scotland at 20 feet high.

no higher than 200 feet above sea level (which was higher in about 1750 BC, when they were carved), and near sources of copper or gold. In Scotland they are particularly plentiful in Argyll at, for example, Baluachraig (153 carvings), Achnabreck (labyrinth connections) and Ballygouran.

The Kilmartin area in Argyll also has cups and cups and rings, with and without tails, on standing stones which, according to Thom, may have performed the important functions of markers on lines along which the midwinter sun rose or set and for forecasting eclipses. In primitive societies these were vital events, and the so-called 'astronomer-priests' who understood them could therefore make dependable forecasts – which gave them great power.

Professor Alexander Thom (1894–1985), who was born in Argyll, produced the first of his groundbreaking books on astroarchaeology in 1967, long after his retirement. For over 50 years he sailed boats in the Western Isles and gained a tremendous knowledge of sites there and all around Scotland. In 1945 he was elected to the Chair of Engineering Science at Oxford; he was never a man to speculate beyond what his measurements and statistics demonstrated. Thom, the definer of the megalithic yard, also showed that the great majority of cup and ring marks, both in Scotland and also further south, employ a unit of measurement which is exactly one fortieth of the megalithic yard used for the erection of elliptical stone rings – which is 0.816 inches.

Over a hundred different theories about their meanings have been proclaimed, but none seem to me to be satisfactory. And what of the radial grooves which often run through the rings, and almost always downhill?

It was probably the Picts in the far north, and in the northern and western isles, who evolved that most Scottish-sounding domestic stone structure, the broch, from the earlier more fortified duns. There are about 550 of them dotted about in those parts, and it would be a fine ambition to visit every one of these fort-like homes (in the manner of Munro-bagging).

Brochs are circular, made with very thick drystone walling, and with surprisingly high single entrances. Inside there were chambers, small yards, central courts and stairways for farmers and their families, beneath a wood or stone roof. The brochs were mostly not much taller than 20 feet or so, but incomplete Mousa rises to over 43 feet on the small island of that name in the Shetland Isles.

The broch of Gurness, north-east of Stromness on Mainland in the Orkney Isles, was unknown until 1930, when it was just a huge green mound with bumps on it. Excavation has revealed that it has little houses with open yards huddled around the now-ruined tower. Midhowe broch on Rousay, Orkney Isles, shows a similar 2,000-year-old habitation pattern with stalled cairns, room for 342 inhabitants with a life expectancy of 25 years.

About nine miles north of Altnaharra (where, incidentally, Britain's coldest-ever winter temperature, -29.2°C, was recorded during the last night of 1995) stands the conical 20-foot-high Dun Dornaigil (sometimes Dundornadilla), and it has a great big triangular stone lintel over the broad doorway.

Brochs were a development, about 2,000 years ago, from the irregularly shaped and fortified duns, found mostly to the west of Scotland. In design and purpose these are reminiscent of the *navetas* of the Balearics, Corsica's *torri* and Sardinia's *nuraghi*.

The dun of Auchteraw on the west side of the River Oich, along the Great Glen Fault, south-west of Fort Augustus, is notable for its vitrified walling, which Thomas Pennant noted at the end of the eighteenth century. The timberwork in the rubble core of its walls had once burnt with such intensity that the rock pieces actually fused together.

There is a holy well, and this is unusual, by the dun at the Braes of Foss about 500 yards north of the road from Kinloch Rannoch and Coshieville, at the foot of Schiehallion in Perthshire.

It is believed that the oldest extant houses in Scotland, and possibly in north-west Europe, are the pair at Knap of Howar on Papa Westray in the Orkney Isles. They are interconnected long houses, and have been dated between 3600 and 3100 BC. All that time ago, somebody carefully planned a kitchen with a central hearth and a living room, divided by thin stone slabs as walls, and an entrance space which would have had a wooden doorway, leading to a farm workshop complete with storage cupboards and shelves. The roof would have been roofed with timber beams and covered with earth and grass. Knap of Howar is not older than Skara Brae which I mention in chapter eight.

St Martin of Tours (c.316–c.397) is the only saint of this name with known connections with Scotland,

The old packhorse bridge at Carrbridge over the River Dulnain.

and so it must be this remarkable miracle-worker who lends his name to Kilmartin in mid-Argyll on the west coast of Scotland. The prefix comes from *cille*, which is Gaelic for 'church'. This lovely old area has an abundance of 'old stones' for us to puzzle upon. And some new discoveries too. It has recently been realised that there may have been an astonishing three-mile-long avenue of stones leading to and from the greatest display there of rock art, which I discussed earlier in this chapter. *Three miles!*

Man has lived for perhaps 6,000 years around Kilmartin, and his legacies are all around. There is the line of five burial cairns. Then there are the three Nether Largies. The capstone on the central cist in the northern one has carved on its underside cupmarks and flat Bronze Age axes. Older than these is the Temple Wood ring of 13 stones – once there were 20 with a diameter of 40 feet – with its large open burial cist at the middle. 'Temple' or 'Teampull' sites are considered by astroarchaeologists to be of special significance. There are many finely carved gravestones at Kilmartin Kirkyard. North lies the four Kintraw cairns, and a standing stone, 13 feet high, south-west of the large

cairn beside the road, which was possibly a Neolithic calculator for midwinter solstices, using mountain peaks on faraway Jura. Eyesight must have been much better in those days.

Rock art in Argyll has been mentioned. The most elaborate and best preserved are at Achnabreck (already mentioned) and Kilmichael Glassary. South of Kilmartin looms the mighty hillfort of Dunadd where carvings, which include a Pictish one of a boar, a famous imprint of a right foot and an Ogham inscription, are assumed to indicate that this half natural outcrop/half man-made construction on the east of Moine Mhor was an important high place. In about the fifth century royal incomers from Dalriada (*Dàl Riata*) in Northern Ireland settled in Argyll, and Dunadd was one of their four great strongholds. In 843 Kenneth, mac Alpin, already king of Dalriada, became overlord of both Picts and Scots. The matrilinear succession system of the Picts ceased, and a monarchy was established from which ours today is descended.

The avenue of stones in Kilmartin is surpassed in grandeur in Scotland only by The Hill O' Many Stanes in Caithness. The site consists of 22 fan-shaped rows

The remarkable setting of stones at Callanish, on Lewis, looking along one avenue (c.1800 BC). The ground steadily rises, away from the village, to the centre.

of more than 200 stones on a south-facing slope. Alexander Thom, who called the place Mid Clyth, showed that the smallish stones must have been set up in about 1900 BC for calculating the moonrise at midsummer and midwinter — a magnificent observatory, in fact.

Balnuaran of Clava is the name of one of the most beautiful groups of cairns in Scotland, and ironically it is to be found in a calm, wooded setting just a few miles from the bloody battlefield of Culloden. It is thought that the Clava chambered cairn, typified here, represents a fine flowering of a type which originated in Iberia or south-western France, then migrated, as it were, north-west to Ireland, east across the Irish Sea to the Firth of Lorne, up the Great Glen to this area, and thence onwards through time to Denmark.

Most chamber tombs in the British Isles have their entrances facing east. Here at Balnuaran of Clava the two passage graves have single entrances on exactly the same south-south-west axis — which points to the midwinter sunset. Between them, but slightly off that line, lies a ring cairn, 104 feet in diameter and kerbed with nine mighty stones, one of them cup marked and three of them attached to the central chamber with three thin earth banks, rather like spokes to a hub cap. In its neighbouring passage graves, cup and cup and ring marks are aplenty.

Just to the west of the central ring cairn lies a small, alluring Bronze Age stone circle, just 12 feet across, at the foot of a tree. Its fellow stones bear cup and cup and ring marks too, and inside excavators have found a strange scattering of fragments of white quartz.

Johnson and his amanuensis James Boswell visited these cairns in 1773. Boswell's recorded observation by Johnson demonstrates that the great scholar did not do enough 'seeing' there. Had he done so, then 'believing' would surely have followed: 'to go and see one druidical temple is only to see that it is nothing, for there is neither art nor power in it; and seeing one is quite enough.' Wrong, Doctor, wrong.

In 1865 Queen Victoria dignified Croft Moraig stone, west of Aberfeldy, in Perthshire, with a visit, and perhaps it is fortunate that we do not have her

Skara Brae, the Neolithic settlement overlooking the Bay of Skaill on Mainland, in the Orkney Islands, dates back to about 3900 BC. It was revealed after a violent storm in 1850.

observations in any detail. The site is important because, like Stonehenge, it has seen several constructional phases, starting with a horseshoe-shaped setting of 14 wooden posts in about 2850 BC. Two settings of huge stones and an earth bank followed over a long period. On top of the supine stone, which lies along the line of the rise of the midsummer full moon at the south-west, are carved 23 cupmarks. White quartz pebbles and fragments have also been found here at Croft Moraig.

These white quartz pebbles have been called 'godstones'. Wherever they occur within Scotland's 5,150 or so stone circles and more than 500 chamber tombs, there are *never* more than seven of them. They have been discovered, for example, by excavators at Monzie, and also in Perthshire at Berrybrae, Castle Frazer; Corrie Cairn and Culsh, in Aberdeenshire, and at Carrimony and Druidtemple, both, like Balnuaran of Clava, in Inverness.

Scotland's only rock-cut tomb has long been famous. It lies on the island of Hoy in the Orkney Isles, and is known as The Dwarfie Stane, which it is not, being 28 feet in length and 14 feet wide. It has a seven-foot-long passage entrance cut into it. As the cells on each side are

so small, the larger being five feet by three feet by two feet six inches high, the name must have referred to a tiny hermitic inhabitant.

While exploring the sites and mysteries mentioned in this chapter, you will use maps. Try placing the edge of a ruler precisely on to an old church, stone circle, well, or the like which you know personally. Then look along the edge and see if three or more ancient sites occur exactly along the line. If they do, draw a line through them with a very sharp pencil. If not, twist the ruler slowly around your chosen site, all the time watching out for three or more such places to appear along the edge. Repeat the exercise often and you will steadily build up a pattern of lines, and some will become long-distance ones. You may find that some cross each other at precisely the same point on the map. If there is nothing marked at that point, go there and you might find . . . well, something of very great age and not previously recorded.

These are not called ley lines, but 'leys'. They were so-named by their original proposer, Alfred Watkins, in the 1920s. This remarkable Herefordshire man was a brewer, inventor, photographer and also a visionary.

Sueno's Stone, near Forres, now protected from the elements. It is Scotland's tallest cross slab, at over 19 feet above the ground.

The Neolithic stone circle in Midmar Kirkyard has been permitted to remain in a more recent burial ground, established in 1914.
As always with recumbent stone circles west of Aberdeen the main stone is about one foot six inches nearer the centre of the circle than the standing stones.
Nobody knows why.

He wrote of leys in his book *The Old Straight Track*:

Imagine a fairy chain stretched from mountain peak to mountain peak, as far as the eye could reach, and paid out until it touched the 'high places' of the earth at a number of ridges, banks, and knolls. Then visualise a mound, circular earthwork, or clump of trees, planted on these high points, and in low points in the valley other mounds ringed round with water to be seen from a distance. Then great standing stones brought to mark the way at intervals, and on a bank leading up to a mountain ridge or down to a ford the track cut deep so as to form a guiding notch on the skyline as you come up. In a *bwlch* or mountain pass the road cuts deeply at the highest place straight through the ridge to show as a notch afar off. Here and there and at two ends of the way, a beacon fire used to lay out the track. With ponds dug on the line, or streams banked up into 'flashes' to form reflecting points on the beacon track so that it might be checked when at least once a year the beacon was fired on the traditional day. All these works exactly on the sighting line. The wayfarer's instructions are still deeply rooted in the peasant mind to-day, when he tells you – quite wrongly now – 'You just keep straight on'.

The most famous single stone in Scotland, The Stone of Scone, or The Stone of Destiny, was once used for crowning ancient Scottish kings, and they say that it was the pillow upon which Jacob had his dream. Tradition has it that the stone was brought over from Ireland by Fergus I to Argyll, possibly to Dunadd, and by Kenneth mac Alpin on to Scone, when the Picts and Scots became united. Edward I had it removed south to Westminster Abbey in 1296 and placed under the Coronation Chair. It was secretly retrieved by Scottish patriots on 25

A view from the centre of perhaps the finest chambered cairn in Scotland, Maes Howe, east of Stromness in the Orkney Islands. The passage seen is 36 feet long, and is viewed from the 15-square-foot central chamber, which has an extraordinary corbelled roof.

Two of the four remaining Stones of Stenness at the dramatic 5,000-year-old site east of Stromness (Orkney). The taller one stands 16 feet six inches above the ground.

December 1950 and taken to Arbroath Abbey — where the first Declaration of Independence from England was proclaimed in 1320. A cushion-shaped sandstone was returned to the Coronation Chair in Westminster Abbey on 13 April 1951, but was the recovered stone a fake? Does the real one lie in a church in Dundee? There are many who say so.

Either way, the 'Stone' left Westminster Abbey, with Prime Minister John Major's blessing, for only the second time in its 700-year history as Big Ben chimed 7 a.m. on 14 November 1996. The 26-inch, 336-pound, reddish-grey block was escorted on its 400-mile journey north by Coldstream Guardsmen,

and entered Scotland over Coldstream Bridge in the Borders. The Stone of Scone was carried through the streets of Edinburgh on an open Land Rover to the sound of a new bagpipe tune entitled 'The Return of the Stone', amid flags and bunting and accompanied by the Royal Commission of Archers, the Queen's bodyguard in Scotland. After a thanksgiving service in St Giles Cathedral, the Stone moved on to the Great Hall at Edinburgh Castle, where Prince Andrew (also a Scottish earl) surrendered a Royal Warrant confirming Scotland's rightful possession of The Stone of Scone (or Destiny). Amen.

Chapter Two

HOLY PLACES, HEALING POWERS

It has been estimated there are in Scotland about 10,000 'religious sites', ranging from cathedrals to barely spottable and then barely recognisable archaeological sites. Most of these are or were buildings which, for all kinds of reasons, have invited people of all denominations, in the words of one Holy Communion line, to 'draw near, with faith'. Now, water seems to run through the whole of Scottish history without ever diluting it, and issuing endless contexts — warfare, fishing, sailing, baptising, curing . . .

Imagine first, though, whether standing in a roofless country chapel or kneeling in a great cathedral, reflecting upon this sixteenth-century creed by John Gau, vicar and translator:

> I trou in God fader almichtine, maker of heuine and yeird, and in Jesu Christ his sone our onlie Lord, the quhilk wes consawit of the halie Spreit and born of Maria virginem he sufert onder Poncio Pilat to be crucifeit to de and to be yeirdit; he descendit to the hel, and rais fra deid the thrid day; he ascendit to the heuine, and sittis at almichtine God the fader's richt hand; he is to cum agane to juge quyk and deid; I trou in the halie spreit; I trou that thair is one halie chrissine kirk and ane communione of sanctis; I trou forgiffne of sinis; I trou the resurrectione of the flesch; I trou the euerlastand liff.

The most famous healing well in the world today is that at Lourdes, which has attracted millions of visitors. The words 'healing' and 'holy' are cognate. One is said to be hale and hearty if the body is well; if the soul is well or healed it is said to be holy. Thus it is no wonder that healing wells and holy wells, such as that at Lourdes, were at one time generally regarded as one. It is not fanciful conjecture to suggest that church wells are at sites where the wells were discovered first and the erection of the churches followed. It is said that beneath most cathedrals there are blind springs below their high altars. Even today we have the christening ceremony — with water that has been sanctified, 'made holy'.

The waters of the lochs, natural springs, 'magic' stones, healing wells . . . they all seem tied so closely to our many, probably very different, deeply felt definitions of that word 'religion', which cause social divisions to this day. There are rich pickings here for controversialists and conspiracy theorists lurking in the shires.

Why, Pontius Pilate was, was he not, born in Fortingall, Perthshire? The Holy Grail is said to be buried in a certain Rosslyn Chapel, which has a Madonna and Child in place of a cross, and strange masonic markings inscribed in the stone. This Rosslyn Chapel, six miles south of Edinburgh, dates from 1446. Its interior is gloriously filled with a plethora of carved flora, fauna, figures, angels, books, flying buttresses and flowers. Such exquisite celebration!

And isn't Edinburgh really Jerusalem?

That one has been around for a very long time — perhaps since verse ten in chapter seven in the Second Book of Samuel was penned by a knowing yet unknown hand.

As mentioned in chapter one, the prefix Kil- comes from the Gaelic *cille*, meaning 'church', and sometimes the three letters are all that remains of a long-gone early site of worship. Learning and worship so often went together, most particularly in the Western Isles, which are most distinguished of course for St Columba, who landed on Iona in 563. He founded a monastic centre which had an influence over the Highlands and islands of Scotland, and indeed most of western Europe, for more than 1,000 years. The Irishman's monks set out over that time to construct monasteries and churches with related premises, and sometimes even simple cells — and often on sites of pre-Christian worship. One ancient church, the only cruciform one in the Outer Hebrides, which has gained great fame is at Rodel in the south of Harris. It was constructed by Alasdair Crotach, a chief of the MacLeods of Dunvegan and Harris. Following a disagreement with James V, he later lived voluntarily in the tower, which must have been cold and lonely.

In Scotland today there are more recent religious establishments of which St Columba may well have approved. However, some do have surprisingly ancient roots.

About six miles south-west of Elgin, in Moray, stands the huge and beautiful Pluscarden Abbey. It is a quite magical place to visit in the quiet hours. To see the white-robed monks going about their devotions is a profound reminder of the often useless pressures on the rest of us inherited from modern life. The abbey was founded in 1230 by Alexander II, a ruthless churchman who ruled Scotland from 1214 to 1249. Pluscarden was his chosen place for the French-based Valliscaulian monastic order; the abbey was later taken over by the Benedictines. The very existence of Pluscarden Abbey today is due to a private cause of the third Marquess of Bute, who purchased the place from the Earl of Fife in 1897.

A notice in the guest wing of the priory at Pluscarden offers a clear memorandum of the vow of silence:

It is one of our most precious possessions – it is also one of the most difficult to preserve. In a world of constant noise, spiritual silence may be a dimension as unfamiliar to you as the Forth! It may even be frightening at first. It is however an indispensable factor for the development of the spiritual life, for it is vital for the spirit of prayer. You have come to make contact with Reality . . . and so you are respectfully asked to do all you can to assist the monks to preserve their silence.

Pluscarden Abbey, or Priory, as both are described around Elgin, is the only medieval monastery in Great Britain still inhabited by monks and still used for its original purposes. Visitors are welcomed to all services, in which the monks use the ancient Gregorian chant. It also has 26 rooms available for those wishing to stay on retreat. The gift shop sells a wide variety of natural products produced by the monks themselves, such as honey, beeswax, wood carvings, skin balms and so on. Working with the hands is an important part of life at Pluscarden. The trick is to observe them while they are at work.

Pluscarden is beside a stream long called the Black Burn. The best view of Pluscarden Abbey is from just beyond it, where the portable loo cabin is, at the entrance to the main drive. Just walk past and look up, and there is the back of the abbey, with the old ruins in front.

The Samye Ling Buddhist Temple at Eskdalemuir in Dumfriesshire was founded in 1968 when the so-called New Age was commencing. In 1992 the temple acquired Holy Island in the Firth of Clyde. The multi-coloured structure with a pagoda and roof made of gold is 14 miles north of Lockerbie. Its name comes from the oldest Buddhist monastery in Tibet, which has been reduced to rubble by the Chinese. Holy Island was an ancient centre of Christianity (and also a popular site for pilgrims until the end of the nineteenth century); the land on their 900-acre site contains a cave once inhabited by a sixth-century Irish hermit, St Molaise.

Buddhism is one of Britain's fastest-growing religions and now has very many thousands of devotees. Buried in the valley of the River Esk this astonishing Tibetan temple has a thriving community. Yet here all is peace and quiet. There is a water garden with white peacocks and ducks and hens. Around the stone shrines supporting marble Buddhas, the noises of the deep countryside merge and mingle with the bronze gong that calls the community to its prayers.

The Findhorn Foundation was founded in 1962 by

Pilgrimages to 'holy' wells have always worried both Church and State authorities. After the Reformation, efforts were once again renewed to have the practice abolished in Scotland. In a 1581 Act of Parliament, mention is made of:

pervers inclination of mannis ingyne to superstitioun through which the dregges of idolatrie yit remanis in divers pairtis of the realme be useing of pilgrimage to sum chappellis, wellis, croces, and sic other monumentis of idolatrie, as also be observing of the festual dayis of the santes sumtyme namit their patronis in setting forth of bain fyres, singing of caroles within aud about kirkes at certane seasones of the yeir.

The christening font outside Foss Church, north of Aberfeldy.

The ancient font in Balquhidder church. Rob Roy lies in the churchyard.

Peter and Eileen Caddy, together with Dorothy McLean, in a conscious attempt to live with attitudes that search for the divine in everyday situations. It is now a world-famous and substantial establishment; the ordinary becomes much less so because of the shared experiences to be obtained there through work. The Foundation, in the third successive village of the same name in the area, is 25 miles east of Inverness near Forres, by Findhorn Bay, a huge and remote future nature reserve.

And then there are the unattended, roofless, windwhistling places, where there haven't been services for centuries, and yet which can stir that ever-present deep undertow of religious imagination which is present in most of us.

Above the east coast village of Pennan in Banff and Buchan, where stood the famous red telephone box in the film *Local Hero*, and on the slope of Gamrie Mhòr, to the west of Gardenstown, there is a ruined stone building called St John's Chapel, said to have been built by the Thane of Buchan in 1004. This was in

fulfilment of a vow to erect a church to St John the Evangelist if help came forth to enable him to defeat the invading Danes. In the ensuing battle three Danish chiefs lost their lives; their skulls were inserted into the wall of the church and remained there for more than 800 years. It is a magical and lonely little place, and you might well be alone after the prolonged and compulsory walk from the car park.

Only two pre-Reformation cathedrals in Scotland survive in working order. They are the Cathedral of St Magnus in Kirkwall, Orkney Islands (which by a 1486 Royal Charter belongs remarkably not to the church but to the citizens of Kirkwall of all denominations) and the Cathedral that is dedicated to St Mungo in Glasgow.

Few facts are known about St Mungo (known also as Kentigern), the patron saint of Glasgow. It seems that he lived *c.*520–*c.*612, although there are reasons for believing the last date is exact. The so-called facts which have come down to us about St Mungo derive from a biography of him written by a Cumbrian monk many centuries later, and its contents perhaps reflect the various cults which arose around him after his passing. Accordingly, he is supposed to be the son of Thenew (variously Theneu), a daughter of a king of Lothian. (But the father?) Once upon a time this daughter was thrown into the sea at Aberlady and floated to the Isle of May and to a small cave called the Lady's Bed, which contains a pool in its floor. After dwelling there for a time she proceeded in the same manner by floating to Culross where she gave birth to the saint. Beside a well next to the Molendinar burn (near today's centre of Glasgow), he had a stone dwelling place. Of this Bishop Forbes wrote in his *Kalendars* of Scottish saints (1872):

> Kentigern's couch was rather like a sepulchre than a bed and was of rock, with a stone for a pillow like Jacob. He rose in the night and sang psalms and hymns till the second cock-crowing. Then he rushed into the cold stream and with eyes fixed on Heaven he recited the whole psalter. Then, coming out of the water, he dried his limbs on a stone on the mountain called *galath*, and went forth for his day's work.

St Mungo, whose name translates as 'dear friend' and who may in reality have been an English princess's illegitimate son, is the supposed founder of Glasgow Cathedral. The Molendinar burn is now culverted near Glasgow Cathedral, beneath which there is a shrine to St Mungo. This crypt was once known as Blackadder's Aisle, though perhaps it should have been called Fergus's Aisle, because the saint had brought the body of Fergus, an anchorite, on a cart drawn by two wild bulls to the site earlier on. There is an inscription in Gothic script on a stone in the roof of the aisle which confirms that its name should be Fergus's Aisle. There was a dean in the cathedral called Roland Blacader in the sixteenth century, but then again there was a high Scottish churchman in the same period called Robert Blackadder, who became Glasgow's Archbishop in 1492.

One of Scotland's earliest churches may have been at Hoddom in the Annandale district, which has a strange sunken stone building linked by a subterranean passage to an underground chamber. That chamber may have been built by St Mungo when he returned from exile in Wales.

Another great contributor to the earliest days of Christianity in Scotland was St Ninian, who established his mission in 397 at Glasserton, near Whithorn on the south-west coast of Dumfries and Galloway. Candida Casa was the name given by him to the site of the first Christian church in Scotland, which he founded in Galloway early in the fifth century. A priory was built over the church in the twelfth century, and this later became the cathedral church of Galloway. There are related carved stones in the museum nearby.

St Ninian's Well near Arbroath is dedicated to the apostle of the southern Picts. This mere trickle is all that is left of the site of an ancient chapel. Christian burials are still to be found nearby, one dating back to the late sixth or early seventh century. The water from this well was considered to cure a wide variety of

Prayer ribbons in Iona Abbey.

A stained glass window in St Andrew's Cathedral, Dornoch, depicting St Gilbert in his boat. The inscription reads: 'He set masons to hew wrought stones to build the House of God.'

diseases. At St Ninian's the museum is open to all. It consists of one large room filled with marvellous Pictish stones which were rescued from the churchyard (the 'kirkyard', of course) on the high knoll just above a row of redstone cottages called Kirkstile. The church today is comparatively modern, but the ancient symbol stones, rescued and now safely confined under cover, are strange, beautiful and mostly inexplicable.

All over Scotland there are to be found wells and springs dedicated to saints. Thus we find saints such as St Andrew, St James, St John, St Matthew, St Paul, St Peter, St Philip and so on well represented. St Michael has springs as well as churches dedicated to him. There was supposed to have been a very early chapel at the top of Castle Rock in Edinburgh dedicated to St Michael; this would have been in accord with tradition which has St Michael's churches on the summits of very high places, such as Glastonbury Tor. There is a very fine medieval church near Linlithgow Palace in West Lothian dedicated to St Michael, which dates back to the fifteenth century and replaced an even earlier one. In the arms of Linlithgow, St Michael is represented with outspread wings and standing on a serpent, the head of which he is piercing with a spear. Triumph over evil.

It was the son of a Kirriemuir weaver, J.M. Barrie, the creator of *Peter Pan* and also *The Little Minister*, who wrote in the latter book: 'Children like to peer into wells to see what the world is like at the other side.'

Around Scotland there are 'specialist' wells to which one would have gone for specific cures. Those with poor eyesight would have repaired to Glass, near the River Deveron, Aberdeenshire. In extremely wet weather the well there fills up and has always been held to have the power of healing. The same was said of St John's Well at Balmanno in Marykirk, Kincardineshire. A well in Kenmore in Glen Lyon, perhaps, was suitable for the repair of eyesight and also toothache. It is said that another toothache well was in Strathspey.

The fact that no birthplace for him other than Fortingall in Perthshire has been recorded anywhere else in the world enlarges the attraction of the tradition that Pontius Pilate was indeed born in Fortingall. *Holinshed's Chronicles* (1577) record that two Roman ambassadors were on a peace mission in Augustus's reign, and visited a King Metallanus in his hunting lodge on a nearby hill, when a son was born to one of them. Today's Fortingall Church was built in 1902

The circular shape of Orphir church (Mainland, Orkney Islands) makes it unique among Scotland's surviving medieval churches. It was possibly inspired by the rotunda of the Church of the Holy Sepulchre (or Resurrection) in Jerusalem, and was mentioned in the Orkneyinga Saga *(1136).*

with the generosity of Sir Donald Currie of Garth, Glen Lyon, where the village of Fortingall lies, along the road from the Coshieville Hotel. Today Fortingall Church is renowned for its somewhat elderly yew tree. The commentary on its surrounding railings reads as follows:

This celebrated yew tree has grown here for many centuries. Just how many no one can say with total accuracy. Distinguished botanists are agreed however that the specimen of the primeval forests in this area must be 3000 years old, as old as the time of King Solomon and it is believed to be *the most ancient piece of vegetation existing in Europe.* [my italics]

Over two centuries ago, its circumference was 56½ feet. Subsequently, its trunk became fragmented and over the years it suffered at the hands of vandals. Hence a protecting wall and the pillars supporting the limbs.

The age of this yew tree was first confirmed in 1870 by Sir Robert Christison, Queen Victoria's physician. He was no doubt interested in the tree because back in 1829 he had written *A Treatise on Poisons* – and the yew tree is said to have medicinal, and indeed curative, properties (possibly for some cancers).

The circumference of the tree was first measured by the early travel writer Thomas Pennant when he visited the previous and ancient church in 1769. It is known that the limbs of the tree fell further away from each other in 1825, after village boys lit their Beltane fires between the two parts.

Three hundred and fifty yards east of the church, embedded in the earth and one third of their heights below it, lie a group of three triangular sets of stones which locally are called Druid Stones; the site today is called Kenmore. In a field opposite the thatched cottages in Fortingall there is a Mound of the Dead (*Cairn Na Marbh*). Within it are the victims of a great plague which occurred in the fourteenth century; they were brought for burial on a sledge which was drawn by a white horse which in turn was led by an old local woman.

The burial ground of the Campbells of Glen Lyon – they who produced the alcoholic Captain Campbell of the notorious Massacre of Glencoe (1692) – is at the end of the village. St Adamnan, biographer of St Columba and Abbot of Iona in 679, ended his days in Glen Lyon church, which is ten miles further along the road in the glen.

Above Fortingall, on the hillside near the old castle of Garth, there is a spring which had two local names: *Fuaran n' Druibh Chasad* ('Well of the Whooping Cough') and *Fuaran n' Gruarach* ('Well of the Measles').

37

Masonic emblems mounted above the Royal Arch public house in the High Street, Montrose.

In 1882 there was an epidemic of whooping cough and all the children in the area were taken to the well. There they took water from it, in spoons made from the horn of a living cow, and were carried further up the hill to a certain stone. They were then administered with the water in the spoons, taking as much as they could in the hope that they regained their health.

One of the Irish St Fillans is connected with a seat made of rock in the parish of Comrie, west of Crieff on Loch Earn in Perthshire. Rheumatism sufferers sat down on this seat and were then dragged, lying on their backs, down the hill by the legs to St Fillan's Spring. This was especially a custom on 1 May and 1 August, upon which days the sufferers walked three times around the spring from east to west. Then followed a lavish consumption of water and a washing in it and also the throwing of a small, white (probably quartz) stone on to the cairn of the saint near the spring. Rags were left hanging nearby by the afflicted, which was (and still is) a common habit at saints' spots.

Another St Fillan gave his name to a pool west of Killin, also in Perthshire, near Tyndrum, which was revered for its effect upon epileptics. After one of them had walked three times around the pool he was plunged into the water, then bound to the font inside

the nearby chapel, and left alone all night. He had strapped to his head St Fillan's Bell, which was locally known as the Bernane.

A similar ceremony used to take place in Loch Maree in the Highland district, where an epileptic or madman was rowed over to take the waters from St Maelrubha's Well on the tiny isle on the loch, where the saint built a church in the seventh century. He was then towed behind the boat three times clockwise around the isle, brought back into the boat, and thereafter tossed out of it again. He was then tied around the waist with a rope and pulled back into the boat. This was done repeatedly, regardless of the sex of the sufferer. This ghastly routine was repeated day after day for several weeks or until results were perceived.

The water level in St Maelrubha's Well varied. The outlook for the sufferer was poor if it was low; if high, the omens were held to be good.

Here are some ancient Scottish cures. To recover the health of a dying baby the liver from a mouse must be fed. This old practice goes right back to early Egyptian times. Shingles could be cured by the application of the blood of a blackcock. Tonsillitis

The 1,000-year-old ruins of St John's Chapel, above Gardenstown, east of Banff.

The ruins of the twelfth-century east front of St Andrew's Cathedral, once a great centre of ecclesiastical authority.

could be cured with a poultice of cow's dung placed on the outside of the throat. Skin rashes were cured with another kind of poultice: of frogspawn. Drinker's gout could be cured by consuming the burnt ashes of a common crow. St Drostan (who arrived in the area in about 575) was reputed to work miracle cures, and these he did in one of the oldest churches in the north of Scotland. This was St Fillan's (again) Aberdour Church, above the burn on the way to Aberdour Bay, in north Aberdeen (not the Aberdour in south-west Fife). It was founded by St Columba and St Drostan landed here.

On the mornings of Beltane, between midnight and one o'clock, Loch na Nàire ('Loch of Shame'), in Sutherland, is said to acquire temporary medicinal properties, the legacy of a local witch many centuries ago.

A clootie well is a place where people visit, leaving behind a piece of rag, otherwise known as clootie. This is in the form of a pilgrimage and a request for help. There is a well-known one at Munlochy on the Black Isle, some 11 miles north of Inverness. These wishing wells also involved drinking the water. It used to be at the beginning of May but now happens all year round – and it is not a good idea to disturb rags and other pieces of material found near a clootie well.

There are sacred wells near churches at Little Dunkeld on the right bank of the Tay, in Perthshire, Musselburgh, east of Edinburgh, and Motherwell in Strathclyde. Here well-dressing does take place on May Day after a session of face-washing in the morning dew.

Just as certain standing stones and stone circles all around the world are associated with fertility rites, so too are certain wells. There are two on Skye, at Elgol and Stromalas, where barren women may ritually imbibe. The water of the latter is said to be so strong that twins are practically guaranteed.

In the matter of fertility, while it is a common superstition in Scotland not to put a pair of shoes on a table, perhaps while cleaning them, in case a death in the family is provoked, there is also an old Dundee saying to be kept in mind by putative fathers with private ambitions: 'If ye want a boy, dae it wi yer buits on.'

This is a centuries-old description by one Dr George MacGeorge, within an account of Glasgow, of the now-vanished St Thenew's Well, near what had by then become St Enoch's Square (both names associated with Glasgow's patron saint, St Mungo):

It was shaded by an old tree which drooped over the well, and which remained till the end of the last century. On this tree, the devotees, who frequented the

well, were accustomed to nail, as thank-offerings, small bits of tin-iron – probably manufactured for that purpose by a craftsman in the neighbourhood – representing the parts of the body supposed to have been cured by the virtues of the sacred spring, such as eyes, hands, feet, ears, and others.

St Catherine's Balm Well used to be at Liberton, near Edinburgh, in the grounds of a monastery. It must have provided an unusual experience, in terms of both sight and smell, to those suffering from skin ailments. Such cures can be purchased by the bottle today. A visitor to this Balm Well in 1700 wrote:

It is of a marvellous nature, for as the coal whereof it proceeds is very apt quickly to kindle into a flame, so is the oil of a sudden operation to heal all scabs and tumours that trouble the outward skin; and the head and hands are speedily healed by virtue of this oil, which retains a very sweet smell.

According to Hector Boece (the Scottish historian, c.1465–1536) the well was created from a single drop of oil which was brought back from the tomb of St Catherine on Mount Sinai by Margaret, Queen of Scotland, married to Malcolm III.

In the town of Cromarty, on the Black Isle, stands Handyside Ritchie's monument to Hugh Miller (1802–1856), one of Cromarty's most famous sons, who became a preacher, stonemason, banker and a geologist of great note. His cottage and birthplace, dated 1711, is now owned by the National Trust for Scotland. He once wrote of the local Fairies' Cradle, in words that sustained growing opposition of churches of the period to superstitions attached to the sorts of holy wells, healing powers and places of cure of which I have written in this chapter. The Fairies' Cradle was, he wrote:

famous for virtues derived from the saint (of St Bennet) like those of the well. For, if a child was carried away by the fairies and some mischievous imp left in its place, the parents had only to lay the changeling in this [stone] trough, and by some invisible process, their child will immediately be restored to them. The Fairies' Cradle came to a sudden end in about the year 1745. It was then broken to pieces by the parish minister, with the assistance of two of his elders, that it might no longer serve the purposes of superstition.

St Bennet's Chapel (he is more commonly rendered as St Benedict today, and the single 'n' version is about) beside which the spring and trough are, is, suffice to say, now in ruins. We have to assume he approved of that demolition, because Miller, as a preacher, staunchly favoured the Free Church.

I believe that those who have sung this, the 23rd Psalm, within Scotland's churches over the centuries have had no problem at all in seeking medical help wherever they could find it. It is 'passing strange' (Shakespeare) that natural cures are now regarded as 'alternative'. Pantheistic sympathies remain strong to this day, and certain beliefs in the old traditions are maintained, regardless of the seemingly mysterious processes involved:

Wha is my Shepherd, weel I ken,
The Lord Himsel' is He;
He leads me whaur the girse is green,
An' burnies quaet that be:

Aft times I fain astray wad gang,
An' wann'r far awa!
He fin's me oot, He pits me richt,
An' brings me hame an' a'.

Tho' I pass through the gruesome cleugh,
Fin' I ken He is near;
His muckle crook will me defen',
Sae I have nocht to fear.

Ilk comfort whilke a sheep could need,
His thootfu' care provides,
Tho' wolves and dogs may prowl aboot,
In safety me He hides.

Chapter Three

THE CELTS

In the first two chapters I have set out examples of just how many fragments of Scotland's man-made ancient past still lie all about us. They are remnants of a civilisation much higher than the pre-Christian Greek and Roman *literati* dared admit. After the Roman annexation started, in AD 43, propaganda commenced . . . the wild, painted, ignorant savages needed saving from themselves. But when the Romans withdrew in 410, the population was as Celtic as they found it – and quite the opposite of ignorant, in remarkable aspects.

'The Celtic Fringe' was once a geographical arc across northern Europe, with Galatia in Asia Minor at one 'end' and Ireland at the other, in the beginning of the Christian era. These tribes were gradually pushed westwards. To escape Roman and German territorial incursions the Belgic tribe, which was Celtic, was the last one to arrive in Britain. Tribes already established in their kingdoms, some from as far back as 2000 BC, included for example the Britons and the Gaels. These Celts were of one linguistic and cultural, not ethnic, race.

Greek historians called them *Keltoi*, from the Celtic *ceilt* (which also gives 'kilt'), all words indicating 'concealment'. The words are probably references to the fact that the Celts were not given to recording in any form of writing their laws, knowledge and scholarship.

By the end of the fourth century BC the different Celtic tribes controlled northern Europe. As the centuries passed, tribal wars never ceased, and the common language gradually fell into disarray. Today the Goidelic- (Gaelic) speaking branch of the old Celts is confined to the Highlands and Western Isles of Scotland, Ireland, the Isle of Man and the Gaelic-speaking area in Nova Scotia. The other branch, Brythonic (*Cymric*, or Welsh), which incorporates the Gaulish and Galatian Celts, is found in Wales, Cornwall, Brittany and the Welsh-speaking area of Patagonia in Argentina. The Scottish and Gaelic alphabet today, as ever, excludes the letters j, k, q, v, w, x, y and z.

☆ ★ ☆ ★ ☆ ★ ☆

Stories to rede are delitabill,
Suppose that thai be nocht but fabill.

This admonitory couplet was written by John Barbour (*c.*1316–1396) in his epic narrative poem *The Bruce*, which appeared in 1375. He was a Scottish poet who was probably born in Aberdeen and eventually became Archdeacon there. He translated legends from Latin, and was apparently the author of a fictitious pedigree of the 'Stewart' line of kings.

It is of course easy for me to propose: *Lean gu dlùth ri cliù do shinnsre* – 'Let us follow in the brave path of our ancestors' – but the eternal problem of verity lies across that path. And the way to proceed along it is to note wobbly notions just in case they set up resonances in folk memories which I most probably have missed. I recommend the caution sometimes found at the start of guide books: 'Inclusion does not imply recommendation.' Note also that a legend is a true story which has become distorted after constant retelling, and that a myth, on the other hand, is an untrue story, though of a religious nature and origin.

The Syrian-born Stoic philosopher Poseidonius (*c.*135–50 BC), nicknamed 'the athlete' because he was such a polymath, wrote much about the Celts in books which are now lost to us. But they *were* read by a number of distinguished historians, who had little to go on for their mighty works, and drew upon his accounts. Diodorus Siculus (fl. after first century BC) was a Sicilian who wrote a history of the world in 40 volumes, from the creation to Julius Caesar's Gallic wars. Strabo (the 'squint-eyed'; *c.*63–*c.*22 BC) was another; he was a Greek geographer and inveterate traveller who put together 47 books, of which only fragments remain. Athenaeus (fl. 200) was a Greek writer born in Egypt. His bequest to us is his *Deipnosophistai* ('Authorities on Banquets') in 15 volumes, two of which survive, together with parts of others, in the form of *symposia*, a literary style initiated by Plato (*c.*428–348 BC).

Much later Nennius, Abbot of Bangor-on-Dee in about 860, and author of a *Historiae Brittonum*, confirmed that he drew his information about the early

One of the majestic Celtic crosses near the Abbey on Iona.

teristics that he hadn't come across before. They were to be perceived among not a class but a category of Celt called the druids.

Caesar: 'The druids' chief doctrine is that the soul of man does not perish but passes after death from one person to another.' In another passage in his *De Bello Gallico* he wrote that druids 'are concerned with religious matters, perform sacrifices offered by the state and by private individuals, and interpret omens'.

Throughout this book, references are made to stone circles (actually ellipses), standing stones, avenues of stones, and such wondrous complexes as the site at Callanish on Lewis. The remains of over 900 recorded stone circles are not regarded all over Britain today as the detritus of a giant Neolithic job-creation scheme; these have been shown to be highly sophisticated calendrical instruments. Caesar again, in his *Commentaries*, on the druids:

> They have much to say about the stars and their motions, about the magnitude of the heavens and earth, about the construction of nature, about the power and authority of the immortal gods . . . they count periods of time not by the number of days, but by the number of nights: and in reckoning birthdays and the new moon and new year their unit of reckoning [counting] is the night followed by the day.

The knowledge that the druids derived, from what we today commonly call 'ancient sites' — of which the greatest in these islands is Stonehenge — and from telescope wells etc., brought powers to them which could have been terribly misused. But in fact a system of making law and their promulgation on high places (the Scottish 'laws'), the memory of them through education, the celebration of them with choirs, and their requirements through courts (so often found in place names at the feet of raised places; you will find them today) were all evolved by the druids long before the Christian era. This is what Julius Caesar found so hard to comprehend. He just couldn't understand, for example, why a man accused of a crime in this country should be presumed innocent until proved guilty. This common law prevails to this day, whereas on the Continent civil law holds a man to be guilty until found otherwise.

Geoffrey of Monmouth (*c.*1100–1154), Bishop of St Asaph and a historian, mentioned Stonehenge in his (now lost) famous *Historia Regum Britanniae* (1135), which was abridged and edited by Alfred of Beverley (*c.*1150) and published as *Historia de Gestis Regum*

Celts from the writings of others as well as ancient monuments. And he felt they were often hard done by: 'I bore about with me an inward wound, and I was indignant that the name of my own people, formerly famous and distinguished, should sink into oblivion and like smoke be dissipated.'

Nennius would have been much taken by Julius Caesar's own account of his Gallic wars, in *De Bello Gallico*, which is still the scourge of Latin students in classrooms today. Gaius Julius Caesar (born 100 or 102 BC; murdered on the Ides, 15 March 44 BC) was a remarkable man: architect, general, jurist, mathematician, orator, philologist and statesman. While he was in Britain for the second time this tall, thin, bald man began to notice among the tribes he was attempting to subjugate sets of behavioural charac-

Britanniae. Although his dates for Stonehenge are wildly wrong (they are much too late), there is the recommendation of Merlin, the prophet, by Tremorinus, Archbishop of the City of Legions, to the British King Vortigern, as being just the man to bring over Stonehenge from (today's) Curragh in Kildare in Ireland by teleportation.

There were other early Latin chroniclers who were clearly indebted to Geoffrey of Monmouth's confusing yet exhilarating book. Layamon (fl. early thirteenth century), an English priest, wrote *Brut* or *Chronicle of England*, a poetic work of some 32,250 lines based partly on Wace's French version of Geoffrey's *History*, in 1235, two years before his death. Roger of Wendover (died 1236), a Benedictine prior in St Albans, wrote *Flores Historiarum*, a history of the world from the Creation to his own times. Matthew Paris (*c.*1200–1259), an English Benedictine, produced *Chronica Majora*, another world history, but one which concentrated on events in England in his lifetime. Writers in English were also keeping Geoffrey's book open in front of them. They included Robert Wace (*c.*1115–*c.*1183), who was born in Jersey and became a canon in Bayeux, who wrote the Anglo-Norman 15,300-line *Roman de Brut* or *Geste de Bretons*, dated at 1155 and a broad translation of the *History*. Alexander Neckham (1157–1217), who was born on the same night as Richard I and brought up with him, reflected knowledge of the Merlin story in verse in his *De Laudibus Divinae Sapieniae, c.*1200.

In 1325, Ranulf Higden (died 1364), another Benedictine monk, finished *Polychronicon*, his Latin prose history of the world from the Creation to about 1342; it was later continued by others on to 1377. In 1387 John of Trevisa (1326–1412), a Cornish academic, translated Higden's work into English. Almost a century later, in 1482, William Caxton (*c.*1422–*c.*1491) brought the chronicle up to date and printed an edition of it. Thus it was that an account of Stonehenge first reached a printed page, and that a wider circulation of its mysteries became possible for the first time.

It was Geoffrey of Monmouth who told of the laws of Dunwal Molmutius, who in 450 BC, according to Strabo, based his laws on the code of the druid Brutus, *c.*1100 BC. Molmutius was the son of Cloton, Duke of Cornwall (which is a dukedom today of Charles, Prince of Wales) and is buried in the sacred druidic White Mound within the Tower of London. He is referred to by Shakespeare in *Cymbeline*, III, i: 'Molmutius made our laws, Who was the first of Britain which did put His

A richly carved Celtic cross in Aberlemno Kirkyard. Both sides are defined in the drawings on page 49.

brows within a golden crown, and called Himself a king.'

King Alfred 'the Great' (849–*c.*900) had the Molmutine Laws transcribed from Celtic so that he could incorporate them into his Anglo-Saxon Code. The following extracts demonstrate the enduring legacy to our ways of life today from druids in the Celtic period:

☆ There are three tests of civil liberty: equality of rights – equality of taxation – freedom to come and go.

☆ There are three causes which ruin a State: inordinate privileges – corruption of justice – national apathy.

☆ There are three things which cannot be considered solid longer than their foundations are solid: peace, property, and law.

A red sandstone cross in the kirkyard at Aberlemno.

☆ Three things are indispensable to a true union of nations: sameness of laws, rights and language.

☆ There are three things free to all Britons, — the forest, the unworked mine, the right of hunting wild creatures.

☆ There are three things that require the unanimous vote of the nation to effect: deposition of the sovereign — introduction of novelties in religion — suspension of law.

☆ There are three civil birthrights of every Briton: the right to go wherever he pleases — the right, wherever he is, to protection from his land and sovereign — the right of equal privileges and equal restrictions.

☆ There are three property birthrights of every Briton: five (British) acres of land for a home — the right of armorial bearings, the right of suffrage in the enacting of laws, the male at twenty-one, the female on her marriage.

☆ There are three guarantees of society: security for life and limb — security for property — security of the rights of nature.

☆ There are three things the safety of which depends on that of the others: the sovereignty — national courage — just administration of the laws.

☆ There are three things which every Briton may legally be compelled to attend: the worship of God — military service — and the courts of law.

☆ There are three things free to every man, Briton or foreigner, the refusal of which no law will justify: water from spring, river or well — firing from a decayed tree — a block of stone not in use.

☆ There are three orders who are exempt from bearing arms: the bard — the judge — the graduate in law or religion. These represent God and His peace, and no weapon must ever be found in their hand.

☆ There are three whose power is kingly in law: the sovereign paramount of Britain over all Britain and its isles — the princes palatine in their princedoms — the heads of the clans in their clans.

☆ There are three sacred things by which the conscience binds itself to truth: the name of God — the rod of him who offers up prayers to God — the joined right hand.

☆ There are three persons who have a right to public maintenance: the old — the babe — the foreigner who cannot speak the British tongue.

The Celts, and the druids among them, promulgated laws and traditions which obtain to this day. Geoffrey of Monmouth wrote of Molmutius in his history: 'He enacted that the temples of the gods, as also cities, should have the privilege of giving sanctuary and protection to any fugitive or criminal, that should flee to them from his enemy.'

The Celtic priesthood was hierarchic in form. First there were the Ovates who were the appointed guardians of sacred rites and practised divination. The Bards were both warriors and poets who sang the praises of the gods, of the mysteries of nature and of national heroes and their deeds. Strabo referred to them as 'hymn makers'. And then, at the top of the sacred tree, were the druids in the supreme pontifical college, wise to the arcane mysteries, and endowed with official rights to instruct upon their knowledge, to pass judgement and to declare both war and peace. There were either two or three Arch-Druids. We still refer today to the plural Holy orders.

Each spring chosen representatives of the Celtic druids travelled to a general assembly, in the form of a court of justice, which was held in a sacred oak forest near Chartres in northern France. Before proceeding to their political deliberations there was the ritual cutting of mistletoe from oak trees more than 30 years old, in the belief that it cured all manner of ills. It was cut with a golden sickle, and the sprigs were gathered into veils and distributed to the heads of families. Back home it was placed in receptacles filled with water from holy wells. In peace time there followed the sacrifice of two white bulls. In times of war condemned men or prisoners-of-war were required to be executed – and this, remember, is a religious assembly.

Colossal figures in human shapes were fashioned from osiers – the Wicker Men – and the victims were inserted for burning at night on a sacrificial pyre.

Celtic druids, with their knowledge of the zodiac, certainly performed idolatrous ceremonies to the stars. On raised places they preached to the elements of which they learned, which they believed were imbued with spirits, and practised hydromancy, geomancy and divination.

The druids gave great strength to the Celts in their resistance to the Romans. 'The bravery of the Britons', wrote Pomponius Mela in about AD 41, 'is due to their doctrine of the immortality of the soul.' And they gave personal strength to those outside their orders through superstition. The word 'druid' may be derived from the Greek roots that give *drus*, 'oak', and *dendron*, 'tree'. The word dru-vid may mean 'thorough knowledge'. These men who could commune with nature were recognised as wise men, and did much to prepare the ground for the early Christians and their Gospel messages.

There were some 20,000 druidic precepts, all enshrined in verse, and all of which had to be 'learned by heart' by novitiates. No knowledge and teaching was written down, and priesthoods took up to 20 years and three successful annual examinations to attain. Some of these precepts were recorded, in fact, by Molmutius, and in the Celtic and Welsh triads. That the number three is regarded as a lucky number today is probably a legacy of Celtic druids' very wide use of it. Here is just one druidic doctrine – and would that it could be taught today: 'The three canons of perspicuity: the word that is necessary; the quantity that is necessary; and the manner that is necessary.'

Druids were shamans or seers, like Biblical prophets, and they interwove the natural and supernatural in their verse teachings. Pliny the Elder (AD 23–79) came to hear of them, and apparently acquired a Druid's Egg – that of a serpent which was once kept suspended in the air by the hissing of serpents – which he believed bestowed great powers on its possessor.

The severed heads of boars, bulls and stags to the druid represented status and fertility. A mounted

Pictish carvings on a (now) leaning stone beside the road near Aberlemno.

stag's head is still a common sight in Scottish homes today – a very long tradition in trophies. In those sacred groves, if a black bull's head was produced at a trial it indicated that a death sentence had been pronounced. In Britain, until recently, when a death sentence was passed in a court of law the judge donned a black cap or piece of cloth. Another very long tradition.

In the Shaft (Crypt) in the Lascaux complex of caves in southern France there is a depiction of a masked shaman lying before a bison; it was made some time between 17000 and 12000 BC.

Now forward in time. The following passage is in accord with Celtic beliefs, but was recorded in North America by Natalie Curtis in 1904. The speaker was Chief Letakots, of the Pawnee Indian tribe:

In the beginning of all things, wisdom and knowledge were with the animals; for Tirawa, the One Above, did not speak directly to man. He sent certain animals to tell men that he showed himself through the beasts, and that from them, and from

A reconstructed Celtic byre in the grounds of Kingussie Folk Museum. Note the drain to the left of the door.

the stars and the sun and the moon, man should learn. Tirawa spoke to man through his works.

In my book *Megalithic Mysteries* I wrote of the astonishing synchronicity of stone circle, chamber and tomb construction all over Europe. Scotland is rich in megalithic remains, but far less so than Denmark (which figures prominently in Scotland's story), which has over 24,000 listed sites. The word 'megalith' was devised by Algernon Herbert (1792–1855), antiquary (and editor of a volume about Nennius), in his book *Cyclops Christianus* (1849); he Anglicised the two Greek words *megas* ('great') and *lithos* ('stone').

In Deuteronomy 27, Moses (and 'the elders of Israel') is dramatically explicit in his statement of the commandments to be written on plastered 'great stones'. Verse 17 gives a grim warning: 'Cursed be he that removeth his neighbour's landmark . . .'

Some claim that the Scythians and Cimmerians, who developed into the Anglo-Saxon, Scandinavian, Germanic, Lombardic and Celtic nations, were the so-called 'Lost Tribes of Israel' who spread, as prophesied, 'among the heathen', following the routes of the old stones or waymarks ('Remove not the ancient landmark, which thy fathers have set'; Proverbs 22:28). In both pre-captivity Israel and pre-Christian Celtic Britain Baal (the Assyrian *bal*), a local god, was worshipped. Both made temples in his honour in sacred groves of oak and on high places. Both performed human sacrifices.

Were the recumbent stones of Aberdeen (described in chapter one) altars, and were they chosen for their natural shape, never being dressed? *Exodus* 20:25: 'And if thou wilt make me an altar of stone, thou shalt not build it of hewn stones: for if thou lift up thy tool upon it, thou hast polluted it.' Why were the natural white quartz pebbles called 'godstones'? Did ceremonies take place four times a year within stone circles?

Each side of the magnificent Celtic cross at Aberlemno.

The Celts had a special regard for their calendar of fire festivals. Imbolc was held on 1 February, to celebrate calving, lambing and the start of sowing. Cocks were sacrificed where three streams met, using only white birds. It was once also the feast of Brigantia, a Celtic goddess of fertility. She was called Brigit in Ireland, where the Christian Church merged her name with that of St Bridget (*c*.450–*c*.523), who founded a famous monastery in Kildare. The early Christians were always careful to 'shade in' the old 'pagan' names and practices with those of their own choice.

On Imbolc the Christians introduced a service of consecration for all the candles and tapers to be used in the year ahead (still a fire festival at a stretch), in memory of the purification of the Virgin Mary. Thus arose the name Candlemas Day, which is still printed in our diaries on 2 February. A Scottish proverb reads:

If Candlemas Day be dry and fair
The half o' winter's to come and mair;

If Candlemas Day be wet and foul,
The half o' winter has gone at Youl.

Beltane (*bealltainn*) is on May Day, the first of the month, when the Celts kindled their bel-fires on hilltops, danced clockwise around them in rings and then drove their cattle through the embers. For the fires the druids used their nine sacred woods; one of these was calton, or hazel, which gave its name to an ancient law hill, Calton Hill in Edinburgh. Rowan trees and mountain ash were planted near doorways to keep out evil spirits. The wood of aspen and thorn was never used for construction as these trees were inhabited by fairies.

On the morning of Beltane (which is not connected with the god Baal) hearth fires in all homes were extinguished, and later relit with burning brands, *samhnags*, from the ritual fires on their hilltops. Then fresh spring water was brought to the boil over the roaring hearth, and sprinkled over the floors of every building in use.

Lughnasa, Lammas Day, on 1 August derives its name from the Old English *hlafmaesse*, 'the loaf mass', from the ancient tradition of offering neighbours bread made from the new season's wheat. It is also said that Lugh was a Celtic god who presided over a harvest festival which lasted many days.

The fire festival of Samhuinn (Samhain in Ireland), or All Saints' Day, falls on 1 November with the celebrations taking place on the previous evening. This is Hallowe'en, the last day of the old Celtic calendar, when witches flew about on their broomsticks (as dressed-up children remind us today), fortunes were told – a relic of druidic divination – and apples were exchanged as gifts bestowing eternal youth. In Celtic times, on Samhuinn itself, ancestor worship and left-to-right sun-worship rituals came into play. The Otherworld beyond became visible and was seen to be a happy place; but those tempted to enter into it would be instantly returned, to become old immediately, and to die.

Again, the early Christians took the Celtic remnants of older rituals. Samhuinn was turned into another festival, with animals offered to St Martin, instead of the Baal, and the Assyrian-Babylonian gods En-lil and Marduk; the latter was the Babylonian god of battle, heaven and earth, light and life itself. Quite a portfolio. There followed St Martin's Mass – thus Martinmas, another traditional Scottish quarter day, on 11 November. On this day you can get 'Martin drunk' (extremely so), because St Martin of Tours (*c*.316–397) was, among other things, the patron saint of reformed alcoholics. The martin, one of the swallow family, migrates annually from Britain on about 11 November – but the connection really is hard to make!

Celtic society was mobile. Those with ability to serve their communities well rose within it, and this did *not* include military achievement. It was more the spiritual dimension that won the chieftainships – and women were by no means excluded. The great warrior Queen Boadicea (or Boudicca; died AD 61) was proof of this down in the south. Below the chieftains, the professional classes and the administrators (nobles) were the travelling tribesmen, lawbreakers and deserting soldiers. The clan assemblies, organised by the nobles, controlled the use of land. In the Celtic world no one owned it; it was held in trust for the common good, which is a humbling notion . . . *La propriété c'est le vol*, and all that. (P-J Proudhon; 1809–1865; French socialist and forerunner of Karl Marx.)

I have written of the Picts, the earliest Celtic Britons, in chapter one, and of their mysterious disappearance after the ninth century, when Christianity was spreading fast. Their enduring monuments are the unique symbol stones, of which there are about 300 remaining, scattered up the eastern seaboard from Fife as far as the Shetland Islands. More than half of them are in museums or on private land. A reading of Anthony Jackson's book *The Symbol Stones of Scotland* (Orkney Press, 1984) reveals an odd and thrilling world, and he reaches some exciting conclusions, in spite of this summary paragraph:

> My position is that the Picts were, indeed, a totemic society and it was only after the Picts had merged with Scots that they emerged into history and into that type of self-accounting that characterises our civilisation. It is precisely at this point in time that *we* [original italics] began to recognise their historic presence. As they must have existed before this time, yet have no *written* [original italics] records of their own and are only mentioned in passing by others, this previous existence becomes a problem for historians.'

As for Celtic art, the museums of Europe hold many wonderful examples in stone and metal, and their great beauty, so often with a narrative tale to tell, should not surprise us, given the high intellectual achievements of the Celts. The intricate, often interwoven, designs are so moving because they really did represent everyday beliefs and rituals.

Probably the earliest known Gaelic prose is in a book discovered in Cambridge University Library in 1860. It had been there since at least 1715, remains there to this day and is known as *The Book of Deer*. It is a Latin manuscript, and has additional notes in the margins in Gaelic by at least five different hands. They refer to Scottish place-names (confirming, for example, the 'Pit-' prefix in Pictish place-names, to which I have referred elsewhere) and to known historical figures. It was written in Deer Abbey, north-east of Aberdeen, probably in the ninth century. The book contains the Gospel of St John and parts of three others, the Apostles' Creed, and a small part of a prayer for the sick.

Which brings us to one of the outstanding figures in Scottish history – St Columba, who founded Deer Abbey in 580 with his nephew Drostan. The abbey is now in ruins. 'The Stone of Deer', a six-foot-high carved Celtic stone, once stood outside the north-west corner of it, but some idiot destroyed it in about 1854. There are also remains of six stone circles in the area, which might explain why the Irish saint was drawn to the site.

St Columba (*c.*521–*c.*597) was born in Donegal and arrived on Iona in a small boat with 12 companions in 563. He is believed to be descended through Irish royal blood: the O'Neills and from Niall of the Nine Hostages. *Colum*, or *Colomb*, is, charmingly for such a holy man (but such is predestination), 'dove' in Old Irish, deriving from the Latin *columba*. He was also known as Colmcille. He built a monastery on Iona and set about converting the heathen Picts across the water on the mainland. One great triumph was in Inverness, where he converted Brude, the high king, but this was not before he had a fierce confrontation with the Arch-Druid Broichan. To impress the king the druid demonstrated his power over nature by drawing milk from a bull, the sacred animal called the *tarbh*, which represented fertility, potency, power, virility and wealth. Beat that, Broichan said. And so the Irish priest turned the milk into wine.

Most of what we know of St Columba's life is derived from Adamnan's biography of him, *Vita Sancti Columbae* (*c.*695). I mention this, and a connection with the western island of Canna, in chapter eight. St Adamnan (variously Adomnan or Ennan; *c.*628–704) was descended from a grandfather of St Columba's, and he was to become the ninth Abbot of Iona in 679. He was later to adopt the Roman order, persuade parts of Strathclyde to do the same, and established the Roman way of calculating the date for Easter and the resurrection.

On Iona St Columba would have come across the Culdees (possibly from the Old Irish *céle dé*, 'servants of God'), who were keen to preserve the austere tenets of early Celtic monasticism. It is supposed by some that the Culdees, Christianised druids, who survived into the fourteenth century as independent hermits or anchorites and latterly as secular canons in newly created dioceses, were originally from Judea. Further, there was a monastery of druids on Iona over 150 years before St Columba arrived in his boat, who were perhaps converted to Christianity by the Culdees.

It is claimed that these Christianised 'refugees from Judea' were the founders of the British Church, and kept well away from the Roman occupiers by establishing their monasteries, churches and colleges in remote areas like Llantwit Major and on inaccessible islands such as Iona, Bardsey and Lindisfarne. Adamnan wrote that St Columba used to say: 'Christ the Son of God is my Druid.'

St Columba's ancestor, Niall of the Nine Hostages, was so called because he demanded and received hostages from five Irish provinces and from four in

Scotia. It was he who changed the name of north Britain to Scotia.

Aidan (died 606) was inaugurated by St Columba as King of Dalriada in about 574, after the saintly priest heard in a dream on three successive nights that Aidan's brother Eogan should be passed over. From Aidan runs the line of succession through the early Celtic kings to James VI of Scotland, also James I of England, and to our present monarch. And so it can be said that St Columba brought to Scotland a Church, through his towering personality, great personal gifts and missionary zeal, and its State, because Dalriada became today's Scotland.

It was not until the eleventh century that the Celtic Church was folded into the Roman Church, but it managed to cling on to some of its old ways, its leased clan-owned lands and the monasteries upon them. King Macbeth (*c.*1005–*c.*1057) felt secure enough to go on a pilgrimage to Rome in 1050, but he chose to be buried on Iona among the many Irish, French and Norse kings who also desired to 'go home'.

Macbeth had been killed in battle at Lumphanan in Mar by Malcolm III (*c.*1031–*c.*1093), 'Canmore' (great chief), eldest son of Duncan I (*c.*1010–*c.*1040). With Malcolm III's arrival on the throne, after he had the heir Lulach assassinated at Essie in Strathbogie in 1058, the great Celtic period was virtually over. Malcolm was educated and brought up in English ways and he believed in the principles of civil inheritance and feudal ways. He took as his second wife Margaret, sister of Edgar the Atheling, claimant to the English throne, and she rigorously adhered to the Roman Church. It was this lady, later St Margaret, who tampered with the old Celtic services and their Gaelic. She did though patronise the Culdee priesthood. Their son David I (*c.*1084–1153) reorganised the Church along Norman lines, abolished the Celtic liturgy and established our present system of diocesan bishops. The Celtic monks were replaced by Augustinians and Benedictines, while the Culdees retreated to their caves.

The druids have never quite gone away. The first chosen chief of The Order of Bards, Ovates and Druids, which was founded in 1717 and still exists, was John Toland (1670–1722) who studied in Glasgow and Edinburgh. In 1696 he published *Christianity Not Mysteries*, which set deists such as himself against orthodox Christianity. The House of Commons ordered all copies to be burnt.

Chapter Four

IF YOU LOOK OVER THERE . . .

Does distance lend enchantment? In Scotland's case the answer must be 'yes', and not least because there is almost always water somewhere in the picture. It was all very well for the irascible Dr Johnson to say that 'the noblest prospect which a Scotsman ever sees is the high road that leads him to England', but the Highlands and islands and indeed the Borders of Scotland confirm the place as an altogether different country, and no mere province suitable for continuing subjugation.

Before the Second World War there stood a signpost outside a Perthshire town that read: 'Kinloch Rannoch ¼ mile, London 484¼ miles.' The town had no need for it after the hostilities ceased, and still keeps itself to itself. In Perthshire and far, far beyond there are wondrous views to experience; even on a long tour there is always a fresh surprise around the bend. (Especially south of Ayr, on the A719 at Croy Brae ('electric brae') where cars travelling downhill appear to be travelling uphill!)

The Highlands are littered with the remnants of drovers' roads, used since before history for the transport of cattle and sheep to markets which were often many hundreds of miles away. For example, up Glen Devon and down Glen Eagles, where St Mungo had a church, goes the route from the Highlands, via Trysts, down to Falkirk – passing the Maiden's Well (where if you sleep, you will never wake up). As you follow the remnants of these old roads, a clear recollection of the horrors of the Clearances, mostly in the early nineteenth century, should be borne in mind.

North Berwick Law, East Lothian, is 500 feet high, and is one of the most dramatic high places in southern Scotland. Traprain Law, where according to legend treasure is buried, is, strangely, the same height above sea level as the former (and they are intervisible). Law in Scotland was always made in high places.

One of the country's most dramatic car journeys starts by the head of Loch Linnhe (through which the Great Glen Fault runs) at Fort William. The original fort there was built in 1655, and the town was later named after William of Orange. As you drive south on the A82 you cannot miss Scotland's highest mountain Ben Nevis (4,408 feet) rearing up on your left, like its name, 'cloudy and snowy'. After you swing left at Loch Leven and Ballachulish, the village of Glencoe comes into view.

The strath just beyond is the probable location of the infamous, botched and ultimately pointless Massacre of Glencoe on 13 February 1692, and it was all because the chief of the MacIan MacDonalds in the area was just too late in swearing an oath of loyalty to William of Orange. A party of men, led by Robert Campbell of Glen Lyon, who was probably drunk at the time, killed 38 people including MacIan and his wife.

The nine of diamonds in a pack of playing cards is often known as 'the curse of Scotland'. The Secretary of State for Scotland at the time of the massacre was John Dalrymple, Master of Stair, and it was he who initiated this act of governmental genocide. His family coat of arms boasts nine lozenges. There is of course another version of this story, which has the Duke of Cumberland writing down on a playing card, the nine of diamonds, his orders for the slaughter of the Jacobites, to the last of them, after Culloden.

Now you pass east through the glen, the National Trust for Scotland's most mighty and terrifying property. Dorothy Wordsworth wrote of Glencoe in her journal in 1803: 'The impression was, as we advanced up to the head of this first reach, as if the glen was nothing. Its loneliness and retirement made up no part of my feelings: the mountains were all in all.' And Charles Dickens recalled that 'it resembled a burial ground of a race of giants'.

You head on east, thankful that the old narrow road is at least made up and you have spare petrol, past the formidable rising mass of Aonach Eagach, known among climbers as 'the Freak Out'.

On a nice day, and armed with powerful binoculars, you can park the car and step out to enjoy one of Scotland's great wildlife parks: the mysteries of natural survival and reproduction, and all for free. Here is a checklist, most probably incomplete, of the flesh, fur and feathers to be spotted in Glencoe: Blackcock, Blackthroated Diver, Blue Hare, Buzzard, Common Shrew, Cormorant, Curlew, Dotterel (rare; three scoring marks instead of one), Fox, Goat, Golden Eagle, Golden Plover, Grouse, Heron, Highland Cattle, Hooded Crow, Kestrel, Long Tailed Field Mouse, Merlin, Mink, Otter, Peregrine Falcon, Pine Marten, Ptarmigan, Rabbit, Raven, Roe Deer, Short Tailed Vole, Snipe, Snow Bunting, Sparrowhawk, Squirrel (double marks for a red one), Stag, Stoat, Swan, Weasel, Wild Cat, Wild Duck.

Now that you know there is more to Glencoe than the massacre, love and loneliness, drive on to the Moor of Rannoch, the scene of a great literary dash for freedom.

Robert Louis Balfour Stevenson (1850–1894), who never used his third forename, wrote *Kidnapped* in 1885 in Bournemouth, famously employing that third name. It has been in print, along with its sequel *Catriona* (1893; titled *David Balfour* in America), since it was published in the following year. The novel's full title on the title page reads as follows:

KIDNAPPED
BEING
THE ADVENTURES OF DAVID BALFOUR; HOW HE WAS KIDNAPPED AND CAST AWAY; HIS SUFFERINGS IN A DESERT ISLE; HIS JOURNEY IN THE WEST HIGHLANDS; HIS ACQUAINTANCE WITH ALAN BRECK STEWART AND OTHER NOTORIOUS HIGHLAND JACOBITES; WITH ALL THAT HE SUFFERED AT THE HANDS OF HIS UNCLE EBENEZER BALFOUR OF SHAWS, FALSELY SO-CALLED: WRITTEN BY HIMSELF AND NOW SET FORTH.

R.L.S. knew his country:

In the Highlands, in the country places,
Where the old plain men have rosy faces,
And the young fair maidens
Quiet eyes.

John Nevil Maskelyne (1839–1917) was a Wiltshire-born watchmaker who flourished as an 'illusionist', or magician, for 31 years in the old Egyptian Hall in London's Oxford Street. His grandson Jasper succeeded him as Britain's leading 'illusionist', and they

This is the famous opening to chapter 22 in Robert Louis Stevenson's *Kidnapped*, first published in 1886, entitled 'The Flight in the Heather: The Moor'.

More than eleven hours of incessant, hard travelling brought us early in the morning to the end of a range of mountains. In front of us there lay a piece of low, broken, desert land, which we must now cross. The sun was not long up, and shone straight in our eyes; a little, thin mist went up from the face of the moorland like a smoke; so that (as Alan said) there might have been twenty squadron of dragoons there and we none the wiser.

We sat down, therefore, in a howe of the hillside till the mist should have risen, and made ourselves a dish of drammach, and held a council of war.

'David,' said Alan, 'this is the kittle bit. Shall we lie here till it comes night, or shall we risk it and stave on ahead?'

'Well,' said I, 'I am tired indeed, but I could walk as far again, if that was all.'

'Ay, but it isnae,' said Alan, 'nor yet the half. This is how we stand. Appin's fair death to us. To the south it's all Campbells, and no to be thought of. To the north; well, there's no muckle to be gained by going north; neither for you, that wants to get to Queensferry, nor yet for me, that wants to get to France. Well then, we'll strike east.'

'East be it!' says I, quite cheerily; but I was thinking, in to myself: 'Oh, man, if you would only take one point of the compass and let me take any other, it would be the best for both of us.'

'Well, then, east, ye see, we have the muirs,' said Alan. 'Once there, David, it's mere pitch-and-toss. Out on yon bald, naked, flat place, where can a body turn to? Let the red-coats come over a hill, they can spy you miles away; and the sorrow's in their horses' heels, they would soon ride you down. It's no good place, David; and I'm free to say, it's worse by daylight than by dark.'

'Alan,' said I, 'hear my way of it. Appin's death for us; we have none too much money, nor yet meal; the longer they seek, the nearer they may guess where we are; it's all a risk; and I give my word to go ahead until we drop.'

Alan was delighted. 'There are whiles,' said he, 'when ye are altogether too canny and Whiggish to be company for a gentleman like me; but there come other whiles when ye show yoursel' a mettle spark; and it's then, David, that I love ye like a brother.'

The mist rose and died away, and showed us that country lying as waste as the sea; only the moorfowl and the peewees crying upon it, and far over to the east a herd of deer, moving like dots. Much of it was red with heather; much of the rest broken up with bogs and hags and peaty pools; some had been burnt black in a heath fire; and in another place there was quite a forest of dead firs, standing like skeletons. A wearier-looking desert man never saw; but at least it was clear of troops, which was our point.

We went down accordingly into the waste, and began to make our toilsome and devious travel towards the eastern verge. There were the tops of mountains all round (you are to remember) from whence we might be spied at any moment; so it behoved us to keep in the hollow parts of the moor, and when these turned aside from our direction, to move upon its naked face with infinite care. Sometimes, for half an hour together, we must crawl from one heather bush to another, as hunters do when they are hard upon the deer. It was a clear day again, with a blazing sun; the water in the brandy bottle was soon gone; and altogether, if I had guessed what it would be to crawl half the time upon my belly and to walk much of the rest stooping nearly to the knees, I should certainly have held back from such a killing enterprise.

Toiling and resting and toiling again, we wore away the morning; and about noon lay down in a thick bush of heather to sleep. Alan took the first watch; and it seemed to me I had scarce closed my eyes before I was shaken up to take the second. We had no clock to go by; and Alan stuck a sprig of heath in the ground to serve instead; so that as soon as the shadow of

shared an ancestor who had illusions about weighing the earth.

That is precisely what the Revd Dr Nevil Maskelyne (1732–1811), Astronomer Royal, set out to achieve in the years 1774–1776 on the sides of Perthshire's loveliest mountain, Schiehallion (3,553 feet), which means 'The Fairy Hill of the Caledonians' on account of its almost perfect conical shape. It is known locally as 'the Maiden's Breast', and the regulars in the nearby Coshieville Hotel enjoy making contemporary proportional comparisons. (This fine old hotel, at the crossroads by Glen Lyon, once served as barracks for General Wade's men while they built a local stretch of his famous roads in 1725–1738.)

Nevil Maskelyne stayed at Coshieville while conducting his inquiries into the weight of the earth. There is a memorial to him beside the Braes of Foss car park, because he did his sums with his plumb lines surprisingly accurately. They were confirmed soon afterwards by the English mathematician Charles Hutton (1737–1823), who also stayed at Coshieville while checking his calculations overnight. Yes, of course you want to know . . . the weight of the earth, according to the latest estimates, is 6,586,242,500,000,000,000,000 tons.

To undertake his observations, Maskelyne set up a hut to hold stores and supplies and so on on the lower steps of Schiehallion, and he had with him an assistant called Duncan Robertson. Unfortunately, late one day this hut was burnt to the ground and in that hut perished a fiddle belonging to Duncan Robertson. The good Reverend Maskelyne promised to send him a new one from London, and after it arrived Duncan was delighted with its very beautiful appearance, the grain of its wood and its sweet tone. And so he composed a song in praise of his new sweetheart, as he lovingly called the replacement. He called it 'the Yellow Lady from London'.

Possession of the fiddle descended down through his family and was after many decades in the possession of another Duncan Robertson. He went off to Australia and left the fiddle in the safekeeping of his mother. One day it was lent to a Rannoch man, to enable him to compete in a great fiddling and dancing competition in Liverpool. Money became short and the fiddle was pawned, and on coming home he encountered the understandable anger of Mrs Robertson. By this time all the neighbours considered 'the Yellow Lady from London' a true possession of the Rannoch area. Money was raised among these neighbours and Alisdair Phiobair, another Rannoch man, was despatched to

Liverpool to redeem the fiddle. On his way back home he fell, and the neck of the fiddle broke. He put a rough screw in as a temporary holding measure, and it was later properly repaired by Duncan Robertson's brother and a turned wooden pin was inserted.

Many years later Duncan Robertson returned from Australia and naturally wanted to see the fiddle. On finding it in such good condition he said to his brother that he could keep it and hand it on to his second son who bore his own name, Duncan. This of course happened, and 'the Yellow Lady from London' can now be seen during the summer in the museum of the Clan Donnachie at Bruar, north of Blair Atholl, in Perthshire.

Schiehallion is one of 277 hills in Scotland which are more than 3,000 feet high, and they are all, with great affection, called Munro. They are named after Sir Hugh Munro, who published his list of them in 1891 and in doing so started a craze whereby it has become the ambition of serious climbers to reach the peaks of them all. The first person to do so was the Revd A.F. Robertson in 1901: 'Nearer, my God, to thee.' In fact there may be a 278th – a hill called Foinaven in Sutherland. It is now believed to stand above sea level at 3,002.6 feet.

You don't climb Munros, you 'bag' them. Munro-bagging is a national sport for unserious mountaineers in the north. Munros range from Ben Nevis (4,408 feet) to Beinn à Chlaidheimh, which is exactly 3,000 feet high; from Ben Hope in northern Scotland to Ben Lomond, just north-west of Glasgow. The climber and author Hamish Brown is clear in the matter of appreciating the business of bagging Munros: 'You should not start out bagging Munros in the expectation of engendering a love of the Scottish outdoors. The love should come first, climbing Munros second.'

On the summit of a remote Munro, Spidean Mialach, it was once apparently the case that one walker met another, and they nodded to each other. One murmured '165', the other muttered '242'. That was their sole exchange.

Muriel Gray has written a book called *The First Fifty: Munro-Bagging Without a Beard*. She entertains her readers with the following opening remarks: 'You remember your first mountain in much the same way you remember your first sexual experience, except that walking doesn't make as much mess and you don't cry for a week if Ben Nevis forgets to phone next

the bush should fall so far to the east, I might know to rouse him. But I was by this time so weary that I could have slept twelve hours at a stretch; I had the taste of sleep in my throat; my joints slept even when my mind was waking; the hot smell of the heather, and the drone of the wild bees, were like possetts to me; and every now and again I would give a jump and find I had been dozing.

The last time I woke I seemed to come back from farther away, and thought the sun had taken a great start in the heavens. I looked at the sprig of heath, and at that I could have cried aloud; for I saw I had betrayed my trust. My head was nearly turned with fear and shame; and at what I saw, when I looked out around me on the moor, my heart was like dying in my body. For sure enough, a body of horse-soldiers had come during my sleep, and were drawing near to us from the south-east, spread out in the shape of a fan and riding their horses to and fro in the deep parts of the heather.

When I waked Alan, he glanced first at the soldiers, then at the mark and the position of the sun, and knitted his brows with a sudden, quick look, both ugly and anxious, which was all the reproach I had of him.

'What are we to do now?' I asked.

'We'll have to play at being hares,' said he. 'Do ye see yon mountain?' pointing to one on the north-eastern sky.

'Ay,' said I.

'Well, then,' says he, 'let us strike for that. Its name is Ben Alder; it is a wild, desert mountain full of hills and hollows, and if we can win to it before the morn, we may do yet.'

'But, Alan,' cried I, 'that will take us across the very coming of the soldiers!'

'I ken that fine,' said he; 'but if we are driven back on Appin, we are two dead men. So now, David man, be brisk!'

Fanciful footwear employed as a boot scraper on the island of Mull, outside Dervaig on the road towards Calgary.

The smallest professional repertory company in Britain, in the grounds of Druimard. The stage of the Mull Little Theatre measures four paces by two.

A rehearsal in the Mull Little Theatre, which, for obvious reasons, specialises in 'two-handers'.

The Cuillins on Skye.

The atmosphere is brooding in Glencoe.

The Cuillins at dusk.

morning.' She also wrote: 'In the same time it takes someone to get from Central London to Heathrow Airport in a Hackney cab with a fascist behind the wheel, I can be cruising over Drumochter Summit well on my way to Heaven.'

That prolific travel writer H.V. Morton once called the Borders 'a queer compromise between fairyland and battleground'. Perhaps he was mindful of Sir Walter Scott's remark about Middle Eildon Hill, near Melrose, from where he claimed to be able to 'point out forty-three places famous in war and verse'.

The Romans called the three peaks in the Eildon Hills *Trimontium*. It is said that after they withdrew, King Arthur led the British against Hengist and the southerners through 12 battles in the defence of Christianity, and after he died he was laid to rest with his knights in a huge cave beneath the Eildon Hills, to await his country's call to come again. Some would argue that there are as many last resting places of King Arthur as there are oak trees in which the fleeing Charles II historically took refuge overnight.

There have been some mysterious aeroplane crashes in Scotland. Take for example the death of George VI's youngest brother, the Duke of Kent, who was fifth in line to the throne. Eagle's Rock, eight miles southwest of the coastal village of Dunbeath in Caithness, in 1942 witnessed a royal puzzle which has never been satisfactorily solved. The Duke was among 15 air staff on board an RAF Sunderland flying boat which crashed near the Rock on its way to Iceland, exactly half an hour after its take-off from Invergordon.

In the middle of that day there was very bad visibility, with heavy mist all around; the crew, though, were extremely experienced and hand-chosen in view of their royal passenger. After take-off the plane had kept to the coastline but then suddenly turned inland, just missed Drudd's Mount, which is 2,000 feet high, and smashed into Eagle's Rock. The King and Queen heard the news at Balmoral. Bodies were soon recovered; the Duke of Kent's was taken to Dunrobin Castle and then on to London.

However, it soon transpired that one body was not yet recovered. It was missing. Had he lived? Yes, he had. There was a formal inquiry into the tragic accident, and the House of Commons heard two months after it that the plane's course was not on the flight plan, and also that it was indeed flying on a course too low to clear Eagle's Rock.

That flight plan has now vanished. Coastal command records of the time give 2 p.m. as the time of the crash, and yet the pilot's clock was found stopped at

Twin waterfalls on Mull.

1.30 p.m., in accordance with the Duke's own stopped chronograph record of the 30-minute flight. And why did Hansard formally record the crash date as 15 August, when in fact it was on the afternoon of Tuesday, 25 August 1942? It is also a fact that most official, public and royal records of this crash have today vanished or been removed from public sight. The spot where the crash took place is today marked by a tall cross, which Marina, Duchess of Kent, could only bring herself to visit many years later.

The hotel at Glenforsa on the island of Mull has a particular bedroom with an association with air crashes. Prince William of Gloucester, who was later to die in an air crash, once stayed in that room; so did his flying instructor who lived locally; and so also did one Peter Gibbs, a most experienced private flyer who was found dead in the most mysterious circumstances on Mull soon after dawn on Christmas Day in 1975. It is strange to note that, for this sudden nocturnal flight, Peter Gibbs had hired the plane from one Ian Hamilton, who two decades previously had been involved in the removal of the Stone of Scone from Westminster Abbey on Christmas Day 1955.

Rudolf Hess, once Hitler's successor-designate, flew alone to Scotland on 10 May 1941, the eve of Germany's attack on Russia (and the same day the House of Commons was bombed). He did *not* crash, but baled out of his ME 110, dressed in the uniform of a flight-lieutenant in the Luftwaffe, only ten miles from his destination of Dungavel, the Hamilton seat – and demanded to be taken to the fourteenth Duke of Hamilton for a personal meeting. Scotland has stood witness to many dramatic historical incidents, but this lonely German had a truly astonishing proposition: a British–German peace treaty, and he claimed that he had an 'idealistic urge'. Hitler knew nothing of his aerial voyage to doom.

Winston Churchill was watching a Marx Brothers film at Ditchley Park on Sunday 11 May that year when he first heard the news. At first he couldn't believe the Duke's account of his first meeting with Hess . . . and why was the Duke chosen for such a role? Apparently because Hess's political adviser, Karl Haushofer, had a son named Albert (later executed by the Nazis) who had met the Duke at the 1936 ('Jesse Owens') Olympic Games.

On 16 May 1941, Churchill noted: 'I approved the War Office proposal to bring Hess to the Tower [of London] by tonight pending his place of confinement being prepared at Aldershot.'

After the Nuremberg Trials, Hess was imprisoned for life in Spandau Prison in Berlin where he died in 1987. Winston Churchill later referred to Hess's 'completely devoted and frantic deed of lunatic benevolence'. A very odd incident . . . and anyway, was he *really* Rudolf Hess?

These opening verses of a little-known poem, 'Auld Scotland's Sabbath Bells', captures the appeal of simple, lasting lives led over a century ago in the Highlands. It was written by James Norval who worked all his life as a weaver in Glasgow; he was born in 1814.

> I like to hear the Sabbath bells,
> Wi' their sweet tinkling soun;
> When sitting on a water side,
> Miles frae the dinsome toun.
> They bring me back life's sunny morn,
> Wi' a' its witching spells;
> The clachan, burn, the yellow corn,
> The sheep along the fells.
> They bring me back a mither's love,

One of Scotland's smallest fishing lochs, on Mainland, Orkney Islands.

A father's fostering care;
On memory's wings I flee awa'
To speel the auld kirk stair.
I stand within that sacred pile,
Where hymns in volume rose,
And peal'd along the sounding aisle,
To soothe the saint's repose.

Something about the cloth industry in Glasgow seemed to inspire poets. Another Glasgow poet was Hugh MacDonald (1817–1860). He was born at Bridgeton and spent most of his working life as a calico block printer in Glasgow. He walked to work and back every day, a total distance of 16 miles, and on the way derived inspiration for his private writings. Here are the first two verses of 'The Bonnie Wee Well', which is one of the best-known of this minor Scottish poet's works. The well bubbles up on the Gleniffer Braes, nearly four miles south-west of Paisley. There is now a commemorative fountain at the place of the well.

The bonnie well on the breist o' the brae,
That skinkles sae cauld in the sweet smile o' day,

And croons a laigh sang a' to pleasure itsel'
As it jinks 'neath the breckan and genty blue-bell.

The bonnie wee well on the breist o' the brae,
Where the hare steals to drink in the gloamin' sae gray,
Where the wild moorlan' birds dip their nebs and tak'
    wing,
And the lark weets his whistle ere mounting to sing.

Rutherglen ('Red Glen') in Strathclyde inspired yet another poet in the cloth trade of the time to turn his quill to verse-making. His first name is not known but he was P. MacArthur, a pattern designer for the cloth trade, and was born in Paisley on the banks of the Levern in 1805.

This is the penultimate verse from his paean of praise to the town he loved, 'The Burgh Toon o' Rutherglen'.

I widna like to speak owre lood,
Nor ca' them over ill or good,
I'd like to say just what I should
Aboot the folks in Rutherglen
Variety's the charm o' life –

MacLeod's Tables on Skye, south-west of Dunvegan Castle, the hereditary stronghold of the MacLeods of MacLeod.

The Eildon Hills, in the Borders, said to be the last resting place of King Arthur (among many other candidates).

Looking east towards Gardenstown from St John's Chapel (see page 39).

A time o' fun, a time o' strife;
Whiles ane wad think war to the knife
Wad be the end o' Rutherglen.
There's monthly fairs in Rutherglen,
To droon their cares in Rutherglen;
The guidwives bake the teuch soor-cake
At Draigle Dubbs in Rutherglen.

There is a word to be said about the two words 'Draigle Dubbs' in the last line. This is a reference to the Draigle Dubbs fair, which was held on the last market day of the year in Rutherglen. Old women assembled in a house chosen for the meeting and sat around in a wide circle around the hearth. They then kneaded what were called 'sour cakes', handing the dough from one to another around and around until it was made as thin as a wafer. It was then baked on the girdle. It is said that this tradition comes down from Old Testament times and was connected with the worship of Baal.

Queen Victoria once said: 'There is a great peculiarity about the Highlands and Highlanders; and they are such a chivalrous, fine, active people.' The key adjective in the passage is 'active'. She thought nothing of riding over 40 miles in one short day on horseback over rough tracks.

She fell for Perthshire when a frequent guest of the Duke of Atholl at Blair Castle, and his staff quickly learnt to make quite sure that a jug of water from the Queen's Well was always in her bedroom. The Well, probably named after Mary, Queen of Scots, is some five miles from the Castle, at the confluence of the River Tilt and *Allt Mhaire*, and it was a spot Victoria loved.

Thomas Pennant wrote in the late eighteenth century of the glen through which the River Tilt ran, north-east of Blair Atholl:

Glen Tilt, famous in old times for producing the most hardy warriors; it is a narrow glen several miles in length, bounded on each side by mountains of amazing height; on the south is the great hill of *Ben y Gloe*, whose base is 35 miles in circumference, and whose summit towers far above others. The sides of many of these mountains are covered with fine verdure, and are excellent sheep-walks; but entirely woodless. The road is the most dangerous and the most horrible I have ever travelled: the narrow path, so rugged that our horses often were obliged to cross their legs, in order to pick a secure place for our

63

Some tradesmen's signs survive from the days when not everybody could read. This gilded mortar and pestle is above a pharmacy in Dunkeld.

3 Castleton Terrace, Braemar, where R.L. Stevenson spent the summer of 1881 and wrote Treasure Island.

feet; while, at a considerable and precipitous depth beneath, roared a black torrent, rolling through a bed of rock, solid in every part but where the Tilt had worn its ancient way.

Queen Victoria kept a daily diary, a journal in its fullest form, for almost the whole of her long life, and this is what she once recorded about her beloved Glen Tilt:

At a little before 4 o'clock Albert drove me out in the pony phaeton till nearly 6. Such a drive! Really to be able to sit on one's pony carriage, and to see such wild, beautiful scenery as we did, the farthest point being only five miles from the house [Blair Castle], is an immense delight.

We drove along Glen Tilt, through a wood overhanging the River Tilt, which joins the Garry, and as we left the wood we came upon such a lovely view — *Ben y Gloe* straight before us — and under these high hills the River Tilt gushing and winding over stones and slates, and the hills and mountains skirted at the bottom with beautiful trees — the whole lit up by the sun and the air so pure and fine; but no description can at all do it justice, or give an idea of what this drive was.

Oh! What can equal the beauties of nature. What joyment in them! Albert enjoys it so much; he is in ecstasies here.

Such a diary entry could only have led to one conclusion, and, sure enough, in 1853 Victoria and Albert completed the purchase of the Balmoral estate, which lies between Ballater and Braemar, from their friend the Earl of Fife, for £31,500. In the next two years the old Gordon residence was torn down and replaced by a castle with 100 rooms in the Scottish-baronial style. It was basically designed by William Smith of Aberdeen, but the Prince Consort greatly influenced every aspect of the designs and building. After all, he was fresh from the triumph of the Great Exhibition down in London in 1851, of which this gifted man was the prime mover.

The Queen's View above Loch Tummel is a great panorama of marvellous scenery stretching westwards as far as the hills of Glencoe and those southwards to Ben Vrackie. It is commonly supposed that it was named after Queen Victoria, who visited it in 1886. The viewpoint over Loch Tummel was in fact already entitled 'The Queen's View', but Queen Victoria recalled in her diary: 'We got out and took tea. This was a long unsuccessful business. The fire would not burn and the kettle would

Rannoch Moor, in all its bleakness.

not boil. At length Brown ran off to a cottage and returned after some little while with a can full of hot water, but it was no longer boiling when it arrived and the tea was not good.' This was after she had noted 'I had not been there in 1844', when The View was apparently first named. It is more likely that Mary, Queen of Scots had admired the view, because it is known that she visited the Atholl region on hunting trips.

If you look over there . . . to Loch Lomond, north-west of Glasgow, you will see the 'Queen of Scottish lakes', the largest there is in the country. It covers nearly 2,709 square miles, is 21 miles long, varies in width from one to five miles and its depth reaches 623 feet. The glory of Loch Lomond is its enclosure by ranges of hills, which include Ben Lomond (3,192 feet) to the north-east, and on the west side the double-peaked Ben Voirlich (3,055 feet and 3,092 feet).

The area around Inversnaid, on the east side, is Rob Roy country. After the Battle of Dalree in 1306, Robert the Bruce is said to have holed up in what is called Rob Roy's Cave and to have planted yew trees on Eilan Vow, one of the 33 islands in Loch Lomond, for a supply of bows for his soldiers.

On another island, Inchlonaig, a mile east of Luss on the west side of the loch, there was a Mesolithic settlement about 7,500 years ago, which makes it one of the very earliest in Scotland.

The southern island of Bonhill is associated with the Scottish novelist Tobias Smollett (1721–1771) who was born locally. He travelled in Europe on account of his health, and was therefore qualified to write in *Humphrey Clinker* (1771):

I have seen the Lago di Garda, Albano, De Vico, Bolsena, and Geneva, and on my honour I prefer Loch Lomond to them all, a preference which is certainly owing to the verdant islands that seem to float on its surface, affording the most enchanting objects of repose to the excursive view. Nor are the banks destitute of beauties which ever partake of the sublime. On this side they display a secret variety of woodland, cornfields, and pasture, with several agreeable villas emerging as it were out of the lake, till, at some distance, the prospect terminates in large mountains, covered with heath, which, being in bloom, affords a very rich covering of purple. Everything here is romantic beyond imagination. The country is justly styled the Arcadia of Scotland.

THE TAKING OF THE SALMON

A birr! a whirr! a salmon's on,
A goodly fish! a thumper!
Bring up, bring up the ready gaff,
And if we land him we shall quaff
Another glorious bumper!
Hark! 'tis the music of the reel,
The strong, the quick, the steady:
The line darts from the active wheel,
Have all things right and ready.

A birr! a whirr! the salmon's out,
Far on the rushing river;
Onward he holds with sudden leap,
Or plunges through the whirlpool deep,
A desperate endeavour!
Hark to the music of the reel!
The fitful and the grating;
It pants along the breathless wheel,
Now hurried – now abating.

A birr! a whirr! the salmon's off –
No, no, we still have got him;
The wily fish is sullen grown,
And, like a bright imbedded stone,
Lies gleaming at the bottom.
Hark to the music of the reel!
'Tis hush'd, it hath forsaken;
With care we'll guard the magic wheel,
Until its notes rewaken.

A birr! a whirr! the salmon's up,
Give line, give line and measure;
But now he turns! keep down ahead,

And lead him as a child is led,
And land him at your leisure.
Hark to the music of the reel!
'Tis welcome it is glorious;
It wanders thro' the winding wheel,
Returning and victorious.

A birr! a whirr! the salmon's in,
Upon the bank extended;
The princely fish is gasping slow,
His brilliant colours come and go,
All beautifully blended.
Hark to the music of the reel!
It murmurs and it closes;
Silence is on the conquering wheel,
Its wearied line reposes.

No birr! no whirr! the salmon's ours,
The noble fish – the thumper:
Strike through his gill the ready gaff,
And bending homewards, we shall quaff
Another glorious bumper!
Hark to the music of the reel!
We listen with devotion;
There's something in that circling wheel
That wakes the heart's emotion!

– Thomas Tod Stoddart (1810–1880),
angler and author of *Angler's Companion to the
Rivers and Lakes of Scotland* (1847). He lived in
Kelso for most of his life.

Chapter Five

HUNTING, SHOOTING, FISHING — AND GOLF

During his travels around the country late in the eighteenth century, Samuel Johnson referred more than once to Scotland's 'naked nature'. It is one of his more acceptable observations . . . mist and rain, heather and midges, mountains and granite, the immense coastline, water gathered everywhere.

In this great outdoors the individual and collective challenges of sport have been boldly met all around the country and in most weathers, with liberal help from those in-bred Scottish characteristics which have produced such fearsome warriors and defenders of their chosen causes. The fighting men in the clans were chosen for their strength and fitness, which gives us the origins of Highland games and gatherings. After the Battle of Bannockburn on 23–24 June 1314 (in which the Scots under Robert the Bruce vanquished the English), the village of Ceres, south-east of Cupar, held a celebration for the safe return of its bowmen. It has had an annual event *ever since*.

The Braemar gathering, every September, is even older. King Malcolm III, 'Canmore' (*c.*1031–*c.*1093), needed a first-class courier (in Gaelic, *gille-ruith*), of fleeting foot, and so he became the first Scottish monarch to organise a gathering. In it there was a race for the men on his shortlist, up to the top of Craig Choinnich (near the village) and down again.

Between the Battle of Culloden in 1746 and 1782, all clan gatherings and displays of the tartan were banned by London, and it was left to the Highland regiments to promote games. When that order was lifted a dance called *Sean Triubhas* was developed. This is Gaelic for 'ancient breeches', and the violent kicking leg movements in the routine reflect a desire to shake off the dreaded trousers. The Highland Fling is meant to recall the movements of a red deer stag. The Sword Dance can be traced back to Roman times, when the crossed swords rested on a shield.

There were stone-throwing competitions. The stone in Gaelic was called the *clach cuid fir*, 'manhood stone', and some can be seen at the Bridge of Potarch, over the River Dee, west of Banchory. Tossing the caber (*cabar* means 'pole') is a fine competition to witness. The caber at Braemar is 19 feet nine inches long and weighs a mighty 132 lb (the equivalent of 60 bags of white sugar).

In England, horse racing is held to be the 'sport of kings', but it is not as prominent in Scottish sporting and social calendars. An unusually early royal sport in Scotland was real or royal tennis, which originated in French monks' cloisters in the twelfth century. Many kings from Alexander III (1241–1286) onwards enjoyed playing the game.

A royal tennis court was built in Falkland Palace in 1539 and still exists today, as the only remaining *jeu quarré* of the earliest French design. It has never been roofed over, which is a bit of a puzzle. In the sixteenth century there were also tennis courts in Edinburgh, Perth (next to which the luckless James I was murdered, as I mention in chapter nine), Stirling, and St Andrews. Today the only other surviving royal tennis court in Scotland is at Troon.

Curling is still popular in indoor venues, but has never been a royal pastime. The Lake of Menteith in Perthshire is where a great north versus south of Scotland winter curling match takes place if the ice approaches one foot thick.

On Iona there is a memorial stone bearing a carving of a *caman* and ball. This early depiction of the game of shinty (Gaelic: *camanachd*) is known to the growing band of supporters of a game which might be the oldest team ball game in Europe to be played by almost the same rules and conditions. The highest shinty cup-final score is Newtonmore 11 'hails', Furnace 3.

Football, by Football Association rules, is much more recent. The Scottish FA Cup has been won 30 times by Celtic; their first win was back in 1892.

The first world cross-country running championships were held on Hamilton Park Racecourse on 28 March 1903. I described Munros, mountains over 3,000 feet high, in chapter four; they have also attracted running baggers. Between 19 April and 25 June 1990, an extremely fit and strong Hugh Symonds bagged all 277 Munros, running between them. Except, of course, that he had to sail to Mull and row across to Skye. The record for the number of Munros climbed in 24 hours is 28, and was achieved by Jon

Broxap in July 1988. A famous annual race is from Fort William's town car park to the top of Ben Nevis, Scotland's highest mountain (4,408 feet), and back down again. The record for that hideous endurance test is a remarkable one hour, 25 minutes and 34 seconds.

'Doing a MacNab' means achieving a feat by a character in John Buchan's 1925 novel *John MacNab*. You have to catch a salmon and shoot a brace of grouse by lunchtime and bag a stag before dinner. If you get a woman as well during the day, you have achieved a Royal MacNab.

One eighth of Scotland is designated deer forest. But since the days of Scotland's most famous ghillie, Queen Victoria's friend and companion John Brown, deer stalking has been in slight decline. Victorians and Edwardians held stalking in higher esteem than grouse shooting and fishing for salmon. And now there are too many deer, overgrazing moorland and upsetting the natural habitat all over the Highlands.

One of the last wolves in Scotland was killed about 150 years ago by a woman near Auchindrain, southwest of Inveraray in Argyll, by the old bridge. Then she died too – of shock; she had merely stabbed it with her spindle. In recent years there has been talk of reintroducing wolves and bears from Europe back into Scotland, to bring down the rising numbers of Europe's largest land mammal, and in particular red deer hinds.

The red deer (*Curvus elaphus scoticus*) is native to Scotland, and there are probably more than 300,000 of them. A hummel, a red deer stag with no antlers, is quite rare. Other deer have been introduced: the fallow, the sika (Japanese, *Curvus nippon*), the Chinese water deer, the muntjac and, of course, the reindeer.

Stags cast their antlers each year, unlike cattle, and then the stags, hinds and knobbers (young stags) chew on them for the value of the calcium. A stag rarely has more than 12 points on its antlers; a 12-pointer with 'cups' of three points on each horn is called a Royal and is greatly coveted.

For his famous painting *The Monarch of the Glen,* Sir Edwin Landseer (1802–1873) found inspiration in Glenfeshie, south-east of Kingussie. At the time he was also having a naughty affair with the Duchess of Bedford in the area.

Stalkers, gamekeepers and ghillies never fail to be moved by the sound of a ululating lovesick stag in the autumn rutting season. Fewer appreciate the deer tripe, *pocha bindhe* (Gaelic for 'yellow bag'), prepared best after the deer's innards have been grallochfrom in burn water.

Roebucks (*Capreolus capreolus*) and does are very vocal, sounding not unlike a Scottish collie dog. For exercise, mating and the sheer fun of it, they run around 'courses' in woodlands, and these are always symmetrical, becoming well defined in circles, ovals and figures-of-eight; they are used only from late July to mid-August. The deer cast their antlers in November.

John Campbell Shairp (1819–1885) was educated at Glasgow University and Balliol College, where he won the Newdigate Prize in 1842. He was principal of United College in St Andrews from 1868 until he became professor of poetry at Oxford, a position which he held between 1877 and 1887. This is *The Haunt of the Deer*, which Shairp rendered from a Gaelic poem *Ben Dorain* by Duncan Ban MacIntyre (1724–1812). The mountain (3,524 feet) is three miles south-east of Loch Tulla and Bridge of Orchy in eastern Argyll. The Gaelic poet was born in Glenorchy, and was a gamekeeper at the foot of Ben Dorain. He was illiterate, and his nature poetry was taken down by the minister's son in Killin.

Hark, that quick darting snort!
'Tis the light-headed hind,
With sharp-pointed nostril
Keen searching the wind:
Conceited, slim-limbed,
The high summits she keeps,
Nor, for fear of the gun-fire,
Descends from the steeps.
Though she gallop at speed
Her breath will not fail,
For she comes of a breed
Were strong-winded and hale.

When she lifteth her voice,
What joy 'tis to hear
The ghost of her breath,
As it echoeth clear.
For she calleth aloud,
From the cliff of the crag,
Her silver-hipped lover,
The proud-antlered stag.
Well antlered, high-headed,
Loud-voiced doth he come,
From the haunts he well knows
Of Bendorain his home.

Ah, mighty Bendorain!
How hard 'twere to tell
How many proud stags

A friendly yet firm warning on Mainland, Orkney.

In thy fastnesses dwell.
How many thy slim hinds,
Their wee calves attending,
And, with white-twinkling tails,
Up the Balloch ascending,
To where Corrie-Chreetar
Its bield* is extending.

But when the mood takes her
To gallop with speed,
With her slender hoof-tips
Scarce touching the mead,
As she stretcheth away
In her fleet-flying might,
What men in the kingdom
Could follow her flight?
Full of gambol and gladness,
Blithe wanderers free,
No shadow of sadness
Ever comes o'er their glee.
But fitful and tricksy,
Slim and agile of limb,
Age will not burden them,
Sorrow not dim.

How gay through the glens
Of the sweet mountain grass,
Loud sounding, all free
From complaining they pass.
Though the snow come, they'll ask

For no roof-tree to bield them;
The deep Corrie Altrum,
His rampart will shield them.
There the rifts and the clefts
And deep hollows they'll be in,
With their well-sheltered beds
Down in lone Aisan-teean.

* *bield*, shelter

Phantoms have been known to stalkers: the Black Dog by Loch Einich (west of Kingussie) near an old bothy, the Spectre of the Boar on the western side of the Boar of Badenoch by the Pass of Druimachder, and the Grey Man of Ben Macdhui, just south of the mighty Lurcher (4,084 feet) in the Cairngorm mountains.

Blue hares (*Lepus timidus scoticus*), known also as arctic or mountain hares, are still seen in the far north where they moult three times, becoming almost white in the winter. Brown hares (*Lepus europaeus occidentalis*), once quite common, favour lower lands. On a day when only 19½ brace of grouse were brought down, 73 hares were shot on 15 August 1938 on my family's (former) estate on Loch Tummel by a party of five including Ralph Richardson, the actor (in a break from *Othello* at the Old Vic).

Also to be spotted on the moors are those excellent swimmers stoats and weasels; the latter are also known as whittrets, mouse-weasels, futterets and game-rats.

Puffins on the island of Staffa.

There are the very hairy wild goats (*Capra hircus*), descended from the ibex, moving in herds, the sexes together (unlike deer). The master billies and nannies rut in late October and the kids arrive in February. As with red deer matriarchy rules.

Wild black cats (*Felis silvestris grampia*) have been spotted in some parts of the Highlands in recent years, and are probably crosses between wild and domestic animals. There is in the museum at Elgin a stuffed example of the Scottish wild cat, which was found at Kellas, south-west of the town. It is now a protected species.

There are perks for gamekeepers, and the most unusual of these are stags' best friends – their pizzles. Each complete set of genitalia weighs up to 2.2 lb and they are much prized in the Far East, after they have been ground together, for their libido-improving properties. The stalkers, gamekeepers and ghillies enjoy their pizzle stories in the bothies over a peaty fire, dram in hand, as they dry out and warm their aching bones.

☆ ★ ☆ ★ ☆ ★ ☆

Two out of three grouse are dead before they become a year old, and much earlier if they fail to consolidate their territories. They are native to Britain, cannot be reared, and their total numbers and quality go in cycles; I have been hearing 'the grouse are not very good this year' a lot in recent years. They are affected by breeding patterns, parasitic diseases like coccidiosis and strongylosis, and predators such as foxes, hooded crows ('hoodies'), stoats, eagles, peregrines and hen harriers.

Here are some strange, traditional 'harvesting' (as they used to be called) dates and other feathery facts. The shooting of the familiar red grouse (*Lagopus scoticus*) takes place between 'Glorious' 12 August and 10 December. Its declining numbers are dependent, along with the threats to its existence mentioned above, on heather or ling (*Calluna vulgaris*) being annually burnt (the 'muirburn') in strips so young shoots and flowers are brought forward. They nest in lined scrapes among them, laying up to eight eggs. After a shoot, grouse should be laid out for collection with their heads facing the wind – as they would have taken off and landed in life.

Black grouse (*Lyrurus tetrix*) can be bagged eight days later, on 20 August, until the same end-date. Early in the day, during March and April, the blackcocks, who are great singers, put themselves through elaborate mating rituals called 'leks' with the grey hens. Much is displayed and uttered.

White grouse (ptarmigan, as they are commonly called) have flourished high in the Cairngorms for thousands of years, and can be shot between the red grouse dates. On 30 August 1888, Thomas, sixth Lord Walsingham, brought down 535 brace with one gun in Yorkshire, which is still a record.

Whether driving, walking up or shooting over dogs you are very unlikely to find capercailzie in your sights. Their name comes from the Gaelic *cabhor-coille*, meaning 'birds of the woodlands'. The caper (*Tetrao urogallus*) became extinct at the end of the eighteenth century, but was reintroduced early in the twentieth century from Swedish stock, and their numbers now stand at around 2,200. You can bag one of them between 1 October and 31 January.

Common snipe can be had between 12 August and 31 January, as can woodcock, with its all-seeing eyes on top of its head (and called 'Timber-doodle-dandy' in the old days). Wood pigeon can be yours any time, but wild duck and geese can be brought down only as follows: below high tide mark: 1 September–20 February; elsewhere: 1 September–31 January.

The fishladder at Pitlochry by the power station. An average of 5,400 salmon go up it each year.

Woe betide you if you shoot a golden eagle. The 450 or so pairs left are fiercely protected and legally so. And the same goes for the migrating osprey (*Pandion haliaetus*), sometimes called a fish-eagle or fish-hawk, which survives on a diet of fish alone (even saltwater fish). There are some 95 pairs of ospreys in Scotland, apparently devolving from a pair which returned from Africa to Boat of Garten in 1954. It is said they can also be spotted and filmed on Loch Spynie, north-west of Elgin, in Glenmore, leading from Aviemore to Loch Morlich, at Insh, north-east of Kingussie, in Strathspey, at Nethy Bridge, south-west of Grantown, and on the Loch of the Lowes, near Dunkeld. Why such locations? I cannot answer the question. Nor can anybody else . . . the fish diet has always been available, so why did they leave, and why have they returned?

In the world there are 130 species of midge, and the Highlands of Scotland are home to 33 of them. It is open to question whether a true Scotsman is immune to the *Culicoides impunctatus*, and whether the wearing of the kilt in the presence of midges first introduced the Highland Fling.

Sir William Lithgow once confirmed from his Argyll estate that which we all know, that the defeat of the Scottish midge, particularly the female of its kind – the curse of the great outdoors – is 'the Everest of entomology'. Now an effective prophylactic may be at hand – *Myrica gale*, oil from the leaves of bog myrtle – to improve upon the cigar, cigarette and pipe smoke that has hitherto been welcome in the butts and on picnic rugs all around the Highlands.

Until the efficacy of the oil is finally proved, try

Weather indicators on the clubhouse wall at St Andrews' Royal and Ancient Golf Club, founded in 1754.

The clubhouse at St Andrews.

The memorial tablet of 'Young Tommy' Morris, the world-famous golfer, in the kirkyard of St Andrew's Cathedral.

Skin So Soft by Avon. But, if you *are* caught out, remember that toothpaste takes the sting out of insect bites.

Nobody seems to know that Scotland is visited annually by four of the seven species of turtle recorded anywhere in the world. They cross over from central and south America and the Caribbean, not to breed, preferring warmer water for that, but simply to feed on what Scotland's sunken larder has to offer. Jellyfish are their favourites.

The biggest of them, and also the most common of them, is the leatherback turtle which can reach ten feet in length and weigh up to a ton. The other visitors are loggerhead turtles, Kemps Ridley turtles and green turtles.

Turtle spotting is not yet a popular hobby, but shark fishing is increasingly so. If you want to catch a shark you have to make up some rubby dubby. This is a completely disgusting concoction. In a bucket never to be used again for any other purpose, put rotten herrings, mackerel and pilchards, all mashed up with a blunt instrument. Add

pilchard oil, blood from a slaughterhouse and, finally, some bran to thicken the mess. Out at sea, where sharks have been sighted, you gradually empty the stuff overboard, on a straight course.

The biggest one ever caught in Scottish waters was a porbeagle shark, caught in March 1993 in Pentland Firth, Caithness, by Christopher Bennett. It weighed 507 lb.

A hundred and fifty years ago there were more than 7,000 boats bringing herrings from home waters. Harbours were constructed and maintained, boats built, sailcloth made, nets woven and the catches transported, sorted, gutted, cured and packed in coopers' barrels. This once-huge industry has now dwindled away.

There is no need any more to believe old wives' tales, such as this 300-year-old one:

There lived in Stonehaven an old woman who was regarded with considerable awe by the seafaring population. Before a voyage it was usual to propitiate her by the gift of a bag of coals. On one occasion, two brothers, owners of a coasting smack, after setting sail, had to return to port through

A bridge over the River Dee, one of Scotland's great fishing rivers.

stress of weather, the storm being due, it was believed, to the fact that one of the brothers had omitted to secure the woman's good offices in the usual way.

The brother who was captain of the smack seems to have been a firm believer in wind-charms, for it is related of him that during a more than usually high wind he was in the habit of throwing up his cap into the air with the exclamation: 'She maun hae something'. 'She', in this case, was the wind, and not the witch, and the cap was meant as a gift to propitiate the storm.

There are more than 425 square miles of freshwater lochs and rivers in Scotland. Here are some of the records achieved in them: Bream, 8 lb 1 oz/3.629 kg, in Castle Loch, Lochmaben, in 1990; Carp, 26 lb 2 oz/11.849 kg, in Duddingston Loch, at the base of Arthur's Seat, Edinburgh, in 1990; Dace, 1 lb 3 oz/0.553 kg, in the River Tweed at Coldstream in 1979; Eel, 5 lb 8 oz/2.495 kg, in Loch Ochiltree, east of Ayr, in 1987; Goldfish, 1 lb 9 oz/0.709 kg, in the Forth and Clyde Canal in 1978; Grayling, 2 lb 14 oz/1.308 kg, in Lyne Water, west of Peebles; Perch, 4 lb 14 oz/2.210 kg in Loch Ard in 1989; Pike, 47 lb 11 oz/21.631 kg, in Loch Lomond in 1947; Roach, 2 lb 11 oz/1.219 kg, in Strathclyde Stillwater in 1987; Tench, 6 lb/1.219 kg, in Lanark Loch. The oldest club is the Ellem Fishing Club, Berwickshire, founded in 1829.

Among freshwater game fish records are: Brown Trout, 19 lb 10 oz, in Loch Awe, Strathclyde, in 1993; Sea Trout, 22 lb 8 oz, in the River Leven, in 1989.

But the mightiest and oldest record of them all is appropriately against the name of Scotland's most famous fish, the *Salmo salar* – the salmon. It was landed as dusk fell late on 7 October 1922 in the River Tay, with rod and line, by Miss Georgina Ballantine. It weighed 64 lb, its length was 54 inches, and its girth was 28½ inches.

Here are extracts from an account of the great event which was published in the *Fishing Gazette* on 21 October 1922. Miss Ballantine was alone with her father in the boat, 'as Melvin, the boatman, had knocked off at 5 p.m.'.

Hugh Ferguson, starter at the Royal Dornoch Golf Club, gets away the last players of the day.

After towing up the boat we started harling, using two rods, the fly 'Wilkinson' on the right, and the dace, which I was plying on the left. The bait was exceptionally well put on with an attractive curl on its tail and spinning along briskly as only Malloch's minnows can spin.

A few turns at the top of 'Boat Pool' as the sun dipped down behind the hill brought no result. Immediately above the 'Bargie' stone Father remarked that we should 'see him here': scarcely were the words spoken when a sudden 'rug' and 'screech' of the reel brought my rod in an upright position. He was hooked! The bait he seized with no unusual violence at 6.15 p.m. and thinking him an ordinary-sized fish, we tried to encourage him to play into the back water behind 'Bargie', a large boulder. Our hopes, however, upon this point were soon 'barkin' and fleein''. Realizing evidently that something was amiss, he made a headlong dash for freedom and flew (I can apply no other term to his sudden flight). Down the river he went in mid-stream, taking a 5-run of about 500 yards before stopping, at the same time carrying with him about 150 yards of line. Quick as lightning the boat was turned, heading down-stream, and soon we overtook and got him under hand and within reasonable distance.

Heading for the north bank, we were in the act of landing about 200 yards above the Bridge when he came practically to the end of the boat. Scenting danger ahead, he again ran out of reach. Leaving the boat, we followed him down, and as chance would have it he passed between the north pier and the bank when going under the Bridge, otherwise we would have been in a dreadful hole.

Not once did he show himself, so we were mercifully kept in blissful ignorance of the monster we were fated to fight to the death.

About 200 yards below the Bridge Father thought it advisable to fetch the boat, as the fish obstinately kept out in the current. Evidently our progress downstream was farther than Father had anticipated, as I immediately got into hot water; 'dinna lat the beast flee doon the watter like that, 'ummin'.

With few remarks and much hand-spitting, we again boarded the boat, this time keeping in mid-stream for fully half an hour. As time went on the strain of this was getting beyond us; the fish remained stationary and sulked. Then we endeavoured to humour and encourage him to the Murthly bank, but he absolutely refused to move.

Again gradually crossing the river we tried to bring him into the backwater at the junction half-way down to Sparrowmuir, where a small break-water juts out. Again no luck attended our movements in this direction, though we worked with him for a considerable time. Eventually we re-crossed over close to the island. By this time darkness had come down, and we could see the trees on the island silhouetted against the sky.

We had hoped by the light of the moon to find a suitable landing-place, but unfortunately a dark cloud obscured her. The fish kept running out a few paces, then returning, but long intervals were spent without even a movement. He inclined always downstream, until the middle of the island was reached, and the light in the cottage window at Sparrowmuir blinked cheerily across the river . . .

By this time my left arm ached so much with the weight of the rod that it felt paralysed, but I was determined that whatever happened nothing would induce me to give in. 'Man if only the Laird or the Major had ta'en him I wouldna' ha' been sae ill aboot it.' Encouraging remarks such as those I swallowed silently. Once I struck the nail on the head by remarking that if I successfully grassed this fish he must give me a new frock. 'Get ye the fish landed first and syne we'll see aboot the frock', was the reply. (Nevertheless I have kept him to his word and the frock has been ordered.) By this time we were prepared to spend the night on the Island.

Tighter, and tighter still, the order came, until the tension was so great that no ordinary line could have stood the test for any length of time. It says much for both line and tackle in playing such an important part. Nearer and nearer he came until I was ordered to change my seat to the bow of the boat, and by keeping the rod upright Father was thus enabled to feel with the gaff the knot at the junction of line and cast. Having gauged the distance, the remainder was easy. I wound the reel steadily until only the cast (length of cast, 3¾ yards) was left. One awful moment of suspense followed – then the gaff went in successfully, which brought him to the side of the boat. A second lift (no small weight, over ½ cwt) brought him over the end into the floor of the boat, Father, out of puff, half sitting on top of him. Reaching for Mr Moir's 'Nabbie', I made a somewhat feeble attempt to put him out of pain, and was afterwards accused of 'knockin' oot ane o' the puir beast's een!' It is unnecessary to describe the homeward journey; I was ordered to remain in the boat while Father towed it up.

Miss Ballantine was 32 at the time, but she caught her first salmon when only eight. Her achievement is the ultimate proof of the facts that women are better with salmon than men, and that the biggest ones they land are male fish. Pheromones are chemical substances giving off a certain scent which varies between men and women. It has been shown that a man's hand in fresh water will affect the salmon's behaviour, whereas a woman's will not. The cast of a 50-lb-salmon which was caught by Miss Lettice Ward on 12 October 1928, also in the Tay, at Alderns, can

be seen in the Kinnaird House Hotel, near Dunkeld. Its length was 51¾ inches and girth 27½ inches.

The eggs of the king of fish are spawned in the autumn, hatch in the spring into an alevins and develop throughout the summer from fry to parr. By the end of the following summer the parr change into the silver blue colour of the smolt and leave fresh water for the North Atlantic. There they stay for between one and five years, before returning all the way to their home river, never to eat again but to spawn. It is an extraordinary life pattern, aided by an astonishing sense of smell and, even more odd, acute eyesight. A final question: if they have no need to eat again, once back home, why are they attracted to bait?

Sea (or brown) trout (*Salmo trutta*) behave in the same way, with the same sensitivities. Bile acid from a cannibalistic trout can affect the behaviour of others in a dilution climate of 1:1,000 *million*. Further details can be obtained from more than 2,500 books on the *salmonidae* family which have been published. The first-ever treatise on fishing first appeared in

A traditional Scottish game larder in Banff and Buchan.

The Wolf Stone, just south of Helmsdale on the A9 towards Wick.

A Bisset automatic darts game scorer in the Garden Arms Hotel in Gardenstown.

printed form from Wynkyn de Worde in 1496. The author was a woman, Juliana Berners.

☆ ★ ☆ ★ ☆ ★ ☆

In March 1457 an act was passed by James II 'that the Fute-ball and Golfe be utterly cryit, and not usit', and this negative reference is the first known reference to a game that Scotland gave to the world. The earliest comments on golfing style and playing techniques appear in a 1687 diary of an Edinburgh medical student called Thomas Kincaid.

There are more than 425 golf courses today in Scotland – perhaps the highest concentration of them in any country. (I am not counting the 'rooftop courses' in Japan!) Some of them go back a long time. These Scottish monarchs played golf: James IV, James V, Mary, Queen of Scots (yes, really) and James VI. Soon golf had joined archery as a pastime, and the two had connections. For example, in 1603 Edinburgh bowmaker William Mayne was appointed by James VI to be his official golf clubmaker.

The oldest golf club is Gentlemen Golfers (now the Honourable Company of Edinburgh Golfers), which held its first competition on 7 March 1744 on what were already called the Links of Leith. The 13 rules by which the players abided on that day hang in the Muirfield clubhouse. Apart from the creation of the superb course, not much has changed at the club; there has never been a lady member, golf shop or club professional, and definitely no souvenirs. In spite of this sporting Calvinism, Muirfield has hosted 11 open championships, of which the first was in 1892.

It is often stated that the Edinburgh Burgess Golfing Society was established earlier, in 1735, but 1773 seems to be a more realistic date.

Up till about 1850, courses had different numbers of holes: Leith had only five of them, North Berwick seven, Musselburgh nine, Prestwick 12, St Andrews 22 and Montrose 25. By 1833 Perth Golfing Society had a royal patron, but in the next year the Society of St Andrews Golfers insisted to William IV that it was more 'ancient' and, anyway, he was also the Duke of St Andrews. It got its way and now the Royal and Ancient Golf Club is known as 'the home of golf'. (Previous names of the town of St Andrews have been Muckross ('boar wood'), Kilrymont ('church on the royal mount'), and Kilrule ('church of St Regulus').)

The first open golf championship was played at Prestwick by eight entrants over 12 holes three times; Willie Park Senior won with a score of 174 – but there was no prize money. Subsequently its oldest winner has been 'Old Tom' Morris (1821–1908) at the age of 46, and the youngest 'Young Tom' Morris at 17. A 'feathery' ball from 'Old Tom's' time was sold at auction in Edinburgh to a Spaniard in July 1995 for £19,995.

Sir Robert Gordon, historian and native of Dornoch, wrote in 1630 that 'about this toun, along the sea coast, there are the fairest and largest linkes or green fields of any pairt of Scotland, fitt for archery, goffing, ryding, and all other exercise; they doe surpasse the feilds of Montrose or St Andrews'. The links at Dornoch had been created by monks who had been transferred from St Andrews.

There are thousands of golfing stories to share in the '19th hole'. I like this one-liner: Mary, Queen of Scots was out playing golf on 10 February 1567 when she first heard of Lord Darnley's murder.

Chapter Six

EDINBURGH'S SECRETS REVEALED

Sir David Wilkie (1785–1841), to be the King's Limner in Scotland in 1823, brought his artist's eye to this observation: 'What the tour of Europe was necessary to see elsewhere I now find congregated in this one city. Here are alike the beauties of Prague and of Salzburg, here are the romantic sites of Orvieto and Tivoli, and here is all the magnificence of the admired bays of Genoa and Naples. Here, indeed, to the poetic fancy, may be found realised the Roman Capitol and the Grecian Acropolis.'

I will not opine as to the origin of the word 'Edinburgh'. The theories are many and diverse, but here is the earliest (in translation), given in 1521, by John Major, or Mair (1469–1550), whom I quote again later in this chapter:

> In the time of the emperor Claudius, a mighty war began between the confederated Scots and Picts on the one hand, and the Britons on the other – a war which lasted without a break for one hundred and fifty-four years. According to our chroniclers, the Romans were aiming, with the help of the Britons, at making the Scots and Picts tributaries to them; which when these people came to understand, they made a fierce attack upon the Romans and the Britons, sparing neither sex, and levelling with the ground some fair cities of the Britons – Agned for one, which, when it had been rebuilt by Heth, the king of the Picts, came to be called Hethburg, and to-day is known to all men as Edinburgh, the royal seat in Scotland.

The original idea for extending Edinburgh across Nor' Loch actually came from James VII (1633–1701) when he was still the Duke of York and residing at Holyroodhouse as his brother's commissioner to the Scottish Parliament in 1680–1682. Sir William Bruce (1630–1710), the Fifeshire-born Palladian architect, worked on the Palace of Holyroodhouse during 1671–1679, became acquainted with the Duke, and was commissioned to produce some designs for an extension of the cramped and confined city.

The Edinburgh-born architect James Craig (1744–1795) won a competition in 1766 for his grid concept for the New Town. The foundation stone for the first house to be built there, in Rose Court, off George Street, was laid on 26 October 1767. The Mound, between the Towns, was formed between 1781 and 1830 with some two million cartloads of rubble from the construction sites in the New Town, covering for ever the stepping stones across the marshland of the Nor' Loch, which had been created as recently as 1470, in defence of the castle.

Along the old lochside, Princes Street was laid out on the route of an old country road once called Lang Gaitt and then Langdykes. It was going to be called St Giles Street (after the city's patron saint), but George III objected; it reminded him of a lowly ward in the City of London. So instead it was named after the future George IV and his brother. Leith Walk, following an old country footpath, was widened for carriages in 1772. Elegant granite-housed streets in the New Town, such as Albany Street, went up about 1820.

Work started on North Bridge in 1765; it collapsed four years later and the present structure was put in place by 1895. Trains were using General or Joint Station from 1847; the name Waverley was later adopted after Sir Walter Scott's novels. During the periods 1868–1874 and 1892–1897 the platforms and tracks became as they are today, and the station is Scotland's largest.

The six-acre Edinburgh Castle, on a rock 443 feet high, is one of the world's great fortified places, and was completely defended until about 1752. The original access was via a flight of steps. Today's esplanade was formed from rubble brought up during the building of the Royal Exchange (now the City Chambers, of which you will read more in this chapter).

The castle first became a royal residence in the eleventh century, the occupants being Malcolm III 'Canmore' and his second wife Margaret. Her chapel, which seats only 20 people, is sited on the highest point on the rock and is the only Norman building left in Edinburgh. The sainted Margaret, granddaughter of Edmund Ironside, was born in Hungary of a German mother, married Malcolm III in 1070, died four days after his assassination in 1093, and is buried in Dunfermline in the abbey she founded with him in 1072. Turgot (died 1115), briefly Bishop of St Andrews, wrote of Margaret, to whom he was confessor: 'She made the king himself very readily inclined to works of justice, mercy, alms and other virtues.' She had the habit of feeding nine orphans each morning, and is to be remembered when we cross the Forth at Queensferry.

No less than a complete book could do justice to Edinburgh Castle, and I confine myself to two unrelated observations. Firstly, recent excavations have revealed that there may have been a settlement on the rock upon which the castle stands in about 1000 BC. Floors, hearths and floor debris tell us this. There might have been a bone working centre there. Roman pottery of a high quality from the Continent has also been found.

My second and final observation is upon the famous Edinburgh Tattoo, and where its strange name comes from. It originates in eighteenth-century Holland (as is today) and closing time in the taverns,

This is probably the worst poem ever to have been published (1887) about Edinburgh. It came from the pen of the inimitable William Topaz McGonagall. His *Poetic Gems* was published in 1890.

Beautiful city of Edinburgh!
Where the tourist can drown his sorrow
By viewing your monuments and statues fine
During the lovely summer-time.
I'm sure it will his spirits cheer
As Sir Walter Scott's monument draws near,
That stands in East Princes Street
Amongst flowery gardens, fine and neat.
And Edinburgh castle is magnificent to be seen
With its beautiful walks and trees so green,
Which seems like a fairy dell;
And near by its rocky basement is St Margaret's well.
Where the tourist can drink at when he feels dry,
And view the castle from beneath so very high,
Which seems almost towering to the sky.
Then as for Nelson's monument that stands on the Calton hill,
As the tourist gazes thereon, with wonder his heart does fill
As he thinks on Admiral Nelson who did the Frenchmen kill.
Then, as for Salisbury crags, they are most beautiful to be seen,
Especially in the month of June, when the grass is green,
There numerous mole-hills can be seen,
And the busy little creatures howking away,
Searching for worms amongst the clay;
And as the tourist's eye does wander to and fro
From the south side of Salisbury crags below,
His bosom with admiration feels all aglow
As he views the beautiful scenery in the valley below;
And if, with an observant eye, the little loch beneath he scans,
He can see the wild ducks swimming about and beautiful white swans.
Then, as for Arthur's seat, I'm sure it is a treat
Most worthy to be seen, with its rugged rocks and pastures green
And the sheep browsing on its sides
To and fro, with slow-paced strides,
And the little lambkins at play
During the livelong summer-day.
Beautiful city of Edinburgh! the truth to express,
Your beauties are matchless I must confess.
And which no one dare gainsay,
But that you are the grandest city in Scotland at the present day!

where Scottish soldiers often found themselves. The cry would go up: '*Doe den tap toe*' — literally, 'turn off the taps'. '*Tap toe*' became a drum or bugle signal summoning soldiers back to barracks for the night, and evolved into an end-of-the-day ritual.

Holyrood Abbey was founded by King David I in 1128, according to legend, in gratitude for his rescue by a supernatural vision of a cross (rood or rude) which appeared between the antlers of an angry stag that was attacking him. An alternative source for the name is that a portion of the True Cross was kept here, given to King David by his mother, the sainted Margaret. The abbey fell into disrepair, but many royal personages were buried here: James V, Lord Darnley, James II and David II. It was in the chapel that Mary, Queen of Scots and Lord Darnley were married and Charles I was crowned.

The Palace of Holyroodhouse was begun by James

The Seal of Edinburgh.

A famous pub 'story' sign on Edinburgh's Royal Mile, on the corner of the Lawnmarket and Bank Street. A terrible tale . . .

IV in 1501. It was enlarged, destroyed and rebuilt several times. The great picture gallery was used by Prince Charles Edward for receptions and balls before he set off on the '45'. The main interest for most people, however, lies in the apartments of Queen Mary, in the oldest part of the palace. It was here that her secretary David Rizzio (or Riccio) was murdered before her eyes in 1566; some believe that this act of barbarous cruelty was deliberately carried out in front of the Queen in order to make her miscarry (she was pregnant with the future James VI/I at the time). The dark stains in the little vestibule are said to be Rizzio's blood. The trumped-up reason, that he was the Queen's lover, has no shred of evidence to back it up, though she was very fond of him and he used to play and sing to her to soothe her in times of trouble. In 1798 a richly inlaid dagger was discovered in the roof of a little lodge in the grounds known as Queen Mary's bath – was this the dagger that struck Rizzio down? In Mary's day there also used to be a lions' den, built against one of the north windows; no one knows what for.

The eventual succession of Mary's son James to the throne of both Scotland and England bore out the truth of her dying father James V's prophecy at her birth:

> Be this the post came out of Lythtgow schawing to the king good tydingis that the quene was deliuerit. The King inquyrit 'wither it was man or woman.' The messenger said 'it was ane fair douchter'. The king ansuerit and said: 'Adwe, fair weill, it come witht ane lase, it will pase witht ane lase' . . . He turnit him bak and luikit and beheld all his lordis about him and gaiff une lytill smyle and lauchter, syne kyssit his hand and offerit the samyn to all his lordis round about him, and thairefter held upe his handis to God and yeildit the spreit.

There is some splendid statuary in Edinburgh, but none stranger than a marble sarcophagus at Craigentinny, north-east of the city centre. It displays the *Song of Moses and Miriam* and *The Overthrow of Pharaoh and his Egyptians at the Red Sea* beneath a pedimented Roman-style vaulted roof. It is there as a monument to William Henry Miller (1789–1848), who was in his time a famed bibliophile (known as 'Measure Miller' because he always carried a measuring stick) as well as a Member of Parliament for 11 years. He built up an unrivalled collection of early Scottish and English literature, and wished to be so remembered (and not for the rumours that he was actually a woman). He left £20,000 in his will for the sarcophagus, with a clear stipulation that he be buried no less than 40 feet beneath it. No body-snatching to be had there . . . so perhaps the rumours were true after all.

The city's most famous — as well as largest — monument is of course to Sir Walter Scott in East Princes Street gardens. It rises 200½ feet up to its topmost decorated Gothic finial, and its foundations go down 52 feet. The great man was carved from a 30-ton block of Italian Carrara marble by Sir John Steell (1804–1891) in 1846 and his pet dog Maida keeps him company. There is a stairway of 287 steps to the top; likenesses of Scott's most famous characters abound. On the capitals of the pillars supporting the vaulted roof over him are representations of some of Scotland's great royal and literary figures.

The Scott Monument was erected opposite St David Street between 1840 and 1844, cost £16,000 and was to the designs of George Meikle Kemp. He was a mostly unemployed stonemason who taught himself to draw and spent most of his time travelling around Europe studying Gothic architecture – but crucially he was once given a lift by Scott in his carriage, and encouraged to visit Melrose Abbey. Kemp was to enter the Scott memorial competition using the name of a medieval stonemason at the abbey, features of which can now be seen in the Scott Monument. Unfortunately, poor Kemp never saw the finished work, because in 1844 he fell into the Union Canal and drowned. Thus he was spared Ruskin's opinion of his work – 'a small vulgar Gothic steeple on the ground' – and he lies buried in St Cuthbert's Kirkyard.

The only statue of Sherlock Holmes in Britain is to be found on the left-hand side at the head of Leith Walk, at 11 Picardy Place, where he was 'born'. Sir Arthur Conan Doyle (1859–1930) studied at Edinburgh Medical School from 1876 to 1881 and qualified in 1885. His father was an eccentric artist, Charles Altamount Doyle, of Irish stock, who painted in and around Edinburgh.

Calton Hill, 329 feet, and Arthur's Seat, 823 feet, are both the results of volcanic eruptions, and were smoothed by the great glacier, grinding west to east in the Ice Age, which also fashioned the Castle Rock, 445 feet, and Salisbury Crags, near the Palace of

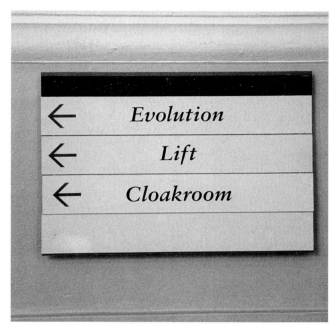

An enigmatic ground-floor sign in the Royal Museum of Scotland in Edinburgh.

A national unicorn rampant, outside St Giles Cathedral in Parliament Square, on top of the Mercat Cross.

One of Edinburgh's many closes, named after the Lord Advocate of Scotland in 1692–1713, Sir James Stewart.

Holyroodhouse. On Calton Hill there is a fine group of monuments, each with a tale to tell.

There is the 102-foot-high Nelson Tower, construction of which took nine long years. Its octagonal basement contains several rooms, and there are stairs up to the parapets. There is more than just a magnificent view from them. There is a time ball set there, a great 5½ feet in diameter, which is controlled by an electric current from Greenwich (it once came from the neighbouring Observatory). A few seconds before 1 p.m. it drops down the outside of the tower and sets off a signal to Edinburgh Castle which causes the one o'clock gun to fire. The time ball, which is similar to the one at Greenwich, was placed there in 1852. It was designed to drop down the outside of Nelson Tower, and was of a sufficient size to be seen from ships in the Firth of Forth, thus enabling their marine chronometers to be regulated.

Not for nothing is Edinburgh known as 'the Athens of the North', and this is in some measure due to the classical architecture of W.H. Playfair (1789–1857). He laid out part of the New Town, designed the National Gallery of Scotland and the Advocates' Library, and enlarged the university buildings. Wherever you look his hand has been, and nowhere more prominently than the Greek revivalist National Monument on Calton Hill, which he designed with C.R. Cockerell (1788–1863). It was conceived in 1816 as a monument to military and naval Scottish heroes who fell in the Napoleonic Wars. Its foundation stone was laid by George IV during his controversial visit in October 1822 and work commenced in 1824. Up went the first stage – 12 magnificent Doric columns, which cost more than £1,000 apiece, with basement and architrave – and then the money ran out. So it is only a third of the planned National Monument.

The other extinct volcano in Edinburgh is Arthur's Seat in Holyrood Park. John Major, or Mair (1469–1550), scholar, theologian, philosopher and historian, who was born near North Berwick and died in St Andrews when he was provost of St Salvator's College, was strongly anti-myth. Yet he wrote the following, in one of the earliest chronicles, *History of Greater Britain, both England and Scotland* (1521); he wrote only in Latin, and this translation (1892) is by Archibald Constable:

what is certain is this, that Arthur, youth as he was, was declared king of the Britons. But his natural endowment was of the noblest; he was fair and beautiful to look on, of a most chivalrous spirit, and none was more ambitious of warlike renown. The Saxons he drove from the island, the Scots and Picts likewise (if we are to credit British chroniclers) he brought under subjection and compelled to obedience. At Edinburgh, in Scotland, was Arthur's kingly seat, and to this day that spot near Edinburgh bears his name.

Arthur's Seat, one of the few mountains in a city, was a natural defensive fort; evidence of Bronze Age terraces and axes has been found there and in Duddingston Loch to the south-east. North of Arthur's Seat, by the artificial St Margaret's Loch, lie the ruins of St Anthony's Chapel, the origins of which are still open to conjecture. You can reach it from

An old doorway in West Bow, near the Grassmarket.

The scholarly figure of Allan Ramsay (1684–1758), poet and editor, watching over Princes Street from the gardens.

Edinburgh's citadel. A flag flies above St Margaret's Chapel, the only Norman building left in the city.

Queen's Drive. Should you then be walking south, still within Holyrood Park, either first easterly around Whinny Hill, or westerly beneath the forbidding Salisbury Crags on Radical Road, then I suggest you head for the Sheep Heid Inn in Duddingston. If you play skittles there you will be enjoying the oldest alley in Scotland — more than 600 years old.

In the wings of history there exists, as I have mentioned elsewhere in this book, a body of people who believe that biblical descriptions of Jerusalem more precisely fit Edinburgh than the Israeli city — and that Arthur's Seat is precisely where the Mount of Olives should be located.

In June 1836 some boys were out rabbiting on Arthur's Seat, and happened upon a small cave. Peering inside they discovered 17 tiny coffins, each just six inches long and carved out of single pieces of wood. The sides were decorated with designs in tin, and the lids were held in place with brass pins. When these were removed, each coffin was found to contain a dressed wooden doll corpse, and they have never been explained.

Mendelssohn's Third Symphony, 'The Scottish', in A minor (Opus 56), was first performed in Leipzig on 3 March 1842, and its beginnings were inspired by his visits to the Palace of Holyroodhouse and Holyrood Park. He was in Edinburgh, before his visit to the Western Isles and Staffa, between 26 July and 1 August 1829. On 28 July he wrote to his family:

It is Sunday when we arrive in Edinburgh; then we cross the meadows, going towards two desperately steep rocks, which are called Arthur's Seat, and climb up. Below on the green are walking the most variegated people, women, children, and cows; the city stretches far and wide; in the midst is the castle, like a bird's nest on a cliff: beyond the castle come meadows, then hills, then a broad river; beyond the river again hills; then blue distance begins; further on you perceive a faint shadow, which they call Ben Lomond.

All this is but one half of Arthur's Seat; the other is simple enough, it is the great blue sea, immeasurably wide, studded with white sails, black funnels, little insects of skiffs, boats, rocky islands, and such like. Why need I describe it? When God Himself takes to panorama-painting, it turns out strangely beautiful. Few of my Switzerland reminiscences can compare to

Where do they go on Sunday mornings? The Boundary is between Edinburgh and Leith.

A statue of John Knox (c.1505–1572), the Reformer, in Parliament Square.

this; everything here looks so stern and robust, half enveloped in haze or smoke or fog.

Many people find a strange resonance about the number 17. Those tiny coffins found on Arthur's Seat were unequal in number, and still inexplicable. What then of the 17 skeletons discovered beneath one of Scotland's oldest chapels, Edinburgh's Magdalen Chapel, hidden beneath George IV Bridge on the Cowgate, as recently as 1992? They included eight children, and were discovered by chance during renovation work on the last Roman Catholic church to be built in Scotland before the Reformation, and the first one to be used for a meeting which led to the establishment of Presbyterianism in Scotland in 1560. The Protestant Reformation Society, which now owns the chapel, says there are no records of burials in what was

originally an almshouse dedicated to St Mary Magdalen.

The chapel itself was built in 1541–45; the four roundels of stained glass in the central south windows depicting heraldic devices are the oldest *in situ* pre-Reformation stained glass in Scotland. Savages' heads can be seen – and quite rightly so, because they were a feature of the arms of the MacQueen family, of whom Michael MacQueen left a bequest of £700 in 1537 so that the chapel could be built.

A variation in numbers. In the 1770s the Scottish Presbyterian Church's meeting house in the old Bristol Street was demolished. Concealed behind wooden panelling around the pulpit were discovered eight skulls of horses. This was an ancient practice to enhance the echo of a preacher's voice.

The short-beaked golden weathercock (fashioned by Alexander Hunyman) on the top of St Giles Cathedral arrived there in 1567, seven years after the medieval furnishings and screens were ripped out from a place of

One of the many ancient wynds of Edinburgh, leading up to the castle.

Lady Stair's Close, with the Writers' Museum on the left.

The wynds and closes of the city have many strange tablets and carvings seemingly unrelated to their present surroundings.

worship dating back to before 850. A few years later the twelfth-century church was divided into four separate churches, and since then it has suffered many depredations, both lapidary and spiritual. In 1638 Dean Hannay was reading from his non-establishment Episcopalian service book when one Jenny Geddes threw a stool at him (both are commemorated by tablets in the Moray aisle). This lowly Tron kail-wife objected very much to the attempt to introduce an English prayer book, and screamed out 'Deil whic the wame o' ye', inviting the Devil to do nasty things to his stomach. It seemed to have worked. Episcopacy was abolished that same year (although restored briefly in 1661), and the church of the Presbyterians became statutory in 1690.

St Giles Cathedral stands in Parliament Square, formerly Close. Once the churchyard extended south to the Cowgate, but now just one tomb remains outside. It is that of the great ecclesiastical reformer John Knox (*c*.1505–1572).

The tall, narrow Thistle Chapel in St Giles Cathedral, designed by Sir Robert Lorimer (1864–1929), honours the Scottish Order of Knighthood. It is also a reminder that the thistle was used as a symbol of the Royal House of Judah of the line of David. I write of this elsewhere in this book.

The Mercat Cross, which stands outside St Giles, was first recorded with this decree in 1447: 'all

patrikis, pluvaris, capons, conynges, chikinnis, and all uther wyld fowlis and tamis be usit and sald about the Merket Croce.' All that time the cross was serving Edinburgh – as a place for business, politicking, royal proclamations, celebration, the pillory and public executions. It has been rebuilt and moved a number of times. The unicorn on top was put there in 1869. Until they were destroyed in 1817, the luckenbooths (enclosed shops) and krames (lean-to wooden booths) against St Giles, and all the trading among them, must have provided a heady and dangerous atmosphere. No wonder that as far back as 1554, according to its Register, the Council ordered 'lanterns or bowets be hung out in the streets and closes, by such persons and in such places as the magistrates should appoint, to continue burning from five o'clock in the evening till nine, which was judged a proper time for people to repair to their respective habitations'. In the Royal Mile, the only street in Edinburgh with five different names, gas lights were placed in the old globes in 1820.

There is a hidden close in the city and few have seen it. And yet it is one of the more remarkable stretches of old Edinburgh still surviving. In 1645 there was a terrible bubonic plague which took thousands of lives, including most of those living in Alexander King's Close, which stretched from the High Street, just east

Sherlock Holmes standing outside his creator's birthplace in Picardy Place.

of St Giles Cathedral, towards Cockburn Street. Mary King was one of the dead, and the daughter of the close's owner, an advocate (in those days closes were named after their owners). She may or may not have returned to haunt the place; either way most of the buildings were sealed up, and the name changed to Mary King's Close. There was a great fire in 1750 which destroyed the old, leaning, multi-storeyed timber buildings completely. Among the tenants dislodged was Andrew Bell, an engraver who, with Colin MacFarquhar, a printer, conceived the *Encyclopaedia Britannica* (launched 18 years later under the editorship of 'Blithe Willie Smellie').

John Adam was commissioned to design a new Royal Exchange to replace Mary King's Close and between 1753 and 1761 the grand building went up, with a large forecourt in front. It is now the City Chambers and has been greatly added to since. On a visit there you would be excused for thinking that the stinking old plague-ridden close has gone for ever. But you would be wrong. For there still exists, beneath the

City Chambers, a 65-yard stretch of the 7-foot-wide cobbled street, complete with a few of the centuries-old shops, probably a wine merchant, a butcher and a baker. It is steep, of course, dropping down 60 feet towards a once-upon-a-time doorway to Craigs Close, Cockburn Street and what would once have been a grassy footpath down to the Nor' Loch.

In these old closes and wynds and among the vennels, life in Auld Reekie was hard. Long before the one o'clock gun first sounded, hand bells rang through the streets at two o'clock in the afternoon; it was the kail bell. Another was rung at eight in the evening and was known as the 'tinkle-sweetie' because it was time for workers to return home. This is Robert Louis Stevenson describing David Balfour's parting with Alan Breck in the last chapter of *Kidnapped* (1886):

> It was coming near noon when I passed in by the West Kirk and the Grassmarket into the streets of the capital. The huge height of the buildings, running up to ten and fifteen storeys, the narrow arched entries that continually vomited passengers, the wares of the merchants in their windows, the hubbub and endless stir, the foul smells and the fine clothes, and a hundred other particulars too small to mention, struck me into a kind of stupor of surprise, so that I let the crowd carry me to and fro . . .

RLS was sensing a city with a past, and doubtless dark deeds.

'Resurrectionist' is not a biblical word. It was used in the eighteenth century to describe the calling of gory beings — body-snatchers — who found a market for their bodily wares in Edinburgh's medical schools. The most infamous of these were two Williams, Burke and Hare, of whom only the former hanged for his hideous troubles. This is what happened.

William Burke (1792–1829) and William Hare (*c.*1790–*c.*1869) came to Scotland from Ulster to find work on the Union Canal some time between 1810 and 1820, while Falkirk was being linked to Edinburgh. Burke and his mistress, Helen MacDougal, took the obvious course of lodging with Hare's wife who ran a lodging house. Seeking extra earnings, they approached lecturer and anatomist Robert Knox (1791–1862) with the notion that he might need more cadavers in his professional day. His positive reply set in motion a series of murders which propelled the names of Burke and Hare into a nasty but remembered corner of Edinburgh's historical past.

For about £10 per fresh body, Burke and Hare set

about fulfilling the dissection requirements of Dr Robert Knox and his unknowing medical students in the Hare lodging house in Tanner's Close, off the then-disreputable Grassmarket.

At first they watched for daily funerals in the graveyards, and on moonless nights they retrieved bodies from freshly turned earth. But the numbers were not high enough, and they turned to murder by almost undetectable suffocation. One evening Burke and Hare enticed two ladies of the night into the lodging house and got them drunk. Mary Patterson passed out, but Janet Brown ran from the house. Mary's body was delivered to Knox the next day, but the two men's fate was sealed with that sixteenth victim. They were arrested on the night of Hallowe'en in 1828 and put to trial, with Janet Brown appearing in court as a witness for the prosecution. The horrible Hare turned witness by her side, and he and his wife were let off Scot-free, so to speak. Margaret Hare fled alone to Ireland. William Hare went south to England, and apparently ended his days as a blind beggar. Burke was hanged by the Mercat Cross on 28 January 1829, slowly, watched by thousands of people. Then, as directed by the case judge, his body was delivered to a medical school for dissection.

The case of Burke and Hare was particularly tasty to the public, but the fact was that public hangings in Edinburgh, between 1770 and 1830, occurred about once an hour, and took about ten minutes each. There are two claimants for the last public execution in the city. The earlier (1864) is 'the Ratho Murderer', George Bryce, son of an innkeeper, who murdered Jane Seaton, a nursemaid, and was hanged in the Lawnmarket. The later (March 1889) was Jessie King, 'the Cheyne Street Baby Farmer', who murdered adopted babies in her lodgings off Raeburn Place.

☆ ★ ☆ ★ ☆ ★ ☆

The Act of Union came into existence on 1 May 1707. Robert Burns (1759–1796), a difficult man but unquestionably one of Scotland's heroes, had a gift, not only for research into folklore, but also for recalling senses of the past. Edinburgh is a city. It is also the capital of a nation-in-waiting, which has been so ever since that distant day of Beltane. Burns wrote this poem in 1792; it should be intoned to the sound of slow and sorrowful music:

Fareweel to a' our Scotish fame,
Farewell our ancient glory;
Fareweel even to the Scotish name,
Sae fam'd in martial story!
Now Sark rins o'er the Solway sands,
And Tweed rins to the ocean,
To mark whare England's province stands,
Such a parcel of rogues in a nation!

What force of guile could not subdue,
Thro' many warlike ages,
Is wrought now by a coward few,
For hireling traitors' wages.
The English steel we could disdain,
Secure in valor's station;
But English gold has been our bane,
Such a parcel of rogues in a nation!

O would, ere I had seen the day
That treason thus could fell us,
My auld gray head had lien in clay,
Wi' BRUCE and loyal WALLACE!
But pith and power, till my last hour,
I'll mak this declaration;
We're bought and sold for English gold,
Such a parcel of rogues in a nation!

Chapter Seven

WEE DRAMS AND THE PUDDIN' RACE

Scotland has a strange larder. In spite of its harsher climate it has originated many more lasting contributions to both taste and table than England, Wales or Ireland. Most of its national dishes and beverages may seem a mite fanciful on the page, but once created their logic becomes clear. They mostly employ readily available basic ingredients, and have evolved for enquiring palates, cold, wet weather, long nights and, of course, completely justifiable national thirsts.

Try saying 'A large Scottish, please'. In some parts of the Highlands you might get executed for that, though never on the Sabbath. Like so many alcoholic drinks, Scotch whisky originated in monasteries at the end of the fifteenth century. Pot stills slowly entered households, and peat fire smoke bestowed the heady tang of cold-defying *uisge-beatha* or *usquebaugh* ('water of life'; Latin: *aqua vitae*), from which the word whisky comes. In spite of the English government's imposition of excise duty after the Act of Union in 1707, private distilleries steadily grew in number. They were banned in 1781, but secret output never ceased, and so the stories of illicit liquor and smuggling were born. The licensed distillers could do little about them until 1823, when severe London government legislation arrived in their support. This had been first proposed in the House of Lords by, of all people, the Duke of Gordon, upon whose estates so many illicit stills operated.

Malt whisky was then created in huge onion-shaped copper pot stills with swan-like necks coiling out of them. These are still lovingly and profitably maintained in many far-flung malt whisky distilleries, and when the inevitable replacements are fitted they are duly endowed with precisely the same bangs, biffs and bumps in their sides as their predecessors. Anything to preserve the unique flavours and tastes, across which Johnson and Boswell came with surprise and pleasure in equal measures. Johnson's amanuensis recorded of one morning: 'Not long after the dram, may be expected breakfast, a meal in which the Scots, whether of the lowlands or mountains, must be confessed to excel us.'

A wee dram, nip, spot or tot is today standardised at 25 ml; in America, when you order a belt, blast, shot, slug or snort of the water of life, at least 50 ml arrives before you. The recorded history of the wee dram began on 28 May 1494 when Friar John Cor placed a large order. It was for 'eight bolls of malt . . . whewith to make aquavitae', broadly equivalent to just over one ton. This order, for Lindores Abbey in Fife, was recorded in the Scottish Exchequer Roll Number 305, and roundly confirms the national habit of imbibing a wee dram as being over 500 years old. The Friar probably produced about 1,400 bottles of the spirit, with which to stoke the inner monk.

Perhaps the good Friar John was attached to the belief that the habit of regular whisky consumption could lead to everlasting life. James Hogg ('the Ettrick Shepherd', 1770–1835) certainly was: 'If a body could just find oot the exac' proportion and quantity that ought to be drunk every day, and keep to that, I verily trow that he might leeve for ever, without dyin' at a', and that doctors and kirkyards would go oot o' fashion.'

After James V of Scotland (1513–1542) married a noble French lady, Mary of Guise-Lorraine, French culinary traditions became fashionable at the Court. Her daughter, to be Mary, Queen of Scots, maintained them. French wines were served, to be followed with French brandy. It took the phylloxera disease in the 1880s, which laid waste to French vineyards, to bring about the substitution of whisky for brandy as the national *digestif*. Nature thus pulled off a neat trick for Scotland's whisky trade, now one of Britain's largest and most constant exports, because today more Scotch whisky is retailed in France in one month than cognac in a year.

Scotch whisky is a distillate, made and matured from elements of cereals, water and yeast, all of which nature replaces. From it comes malt whisky and grain whisky. There are four kinds of malt: the Lowland ones come from an imaginary line between Dundee and Greenock, Highland malt whiskies are made north of that line, Islay malts naturally come from that island. Speyside malt whiskies also come from the designated High-

ACT IV, SCENE I of *Macbeth*, by William Shakespeare

A Cavern. In the middle, a boiling Cauldron. Thunder.
Enter the three Witches.
First Witch. Thrice the brinded cat hath mew'd.
Sec. Witch. Thrice and once the hedge-pig whin'd.
Third Witch. Harpier cries: 'Tis time, 'tis time.
First Witch. Round about the cauldron go;
In the poison'd entrails throw.
Toad, that under cold stone
Days and nights hast thirty-one
Swelt'red venom sleeping got,
Boil thou first i' th' charmed pot.
All. Double, double toil and trouble;
Fire burn and cauldron bubble.
Sec. Witch. Fillet of a fenny snake,
In the cauldron boil and bake;
Eye of newt, and toe of frog,
Wool of bat, and tongue of dog,
Adder's fork, and blind-worm's sting,
Lizard's leg, and howlet's wing,
For a charm of pow'rful trouble,
Like a hell-broth boil and bubble.
All. Double, double toil and trouble;
Fire burn and cauldron bubble.
Third Witch. Scale of dragon, tooth of wolf,
Witches' mummy, maw and gulf
Of the ravin'd salt-sea shark,
Root of hemlock digg'd i' th' dark,
Liver of blaspheming Jew,
Gall of goat, and slips of yew
Silver'd in the moon's eclipse,
Nose of Turk, and Tartar's lips,
Finger of birth-strangled babe
Ditch-deliver'd by a drab,
Make the gruel thick and slab;
Add thereto a tiger's chaudron,

For th' ingredience of our cauldron.
All. Double, double toil and trouble;
Fire burn and cauldron bubble.
Sec. Witch. Cool it with a baboon's blood,
Then the charm is firm and good.

Enter HECATE.
Hecate. O! well done! I commend your pains,
And every one shall share i' th' gains,
And now about the cauldron sing,
Like elves and fairies in a ring,
Enchanting all that you put in.
[*Music and a song,* 'Black Spirits, *&c.' Exit Hecate*]
Sec. Witch. By the pricking of my thumbs,
Something wicked this way comes.
Open, locks, Whoever knocks.

Enter MACBETH.
Macbeth. How now, you secret, black, and midnight hags!
What is't you do?
All. A deed without a name.

lands area, the long winding valley of the River Spey, but they are classified separately because of their distinctly local and individually promotable characters.

Grain distilleries are, with a single exception, located in central Scotland near Edinburgh and Glasgow, where alarming scales of consumption are happily located. Single grain whiskies are growing in popularity. Malt and grain whiskies are brought together in hundreds of different blends (each of which may contain between 15 and 50 different single whiskies); together they account for 95 per cent of world sales of what is termed 'the cup o' kindness' in 'Auld Lang Syne'. The least palatable fact about Scotch whisky is that about 70 per cent of the retail price of a bottle goes to the government in excise duty and tax. The most palatable fact is that no whisky can be sold as 'Scotch Whisky' until it has matured for at least three years (there are no such rules for gin, vodka and liqueurs). If a bottle label states an age, that is the age of the youngest whisky in the blend.

Until the arrival in the 1740s of Clark's hydrometer for proof testing and Bartholomew Sikes's improved version of it in 1818, proof strength was tested with

The wholesale and export price list of James Keiller & Son for August 1892. This long-established marmalade maker flourished under James Michael Keiller (1851–1899).

gunpowder. It was mixed with the whisky and ignited. If the gunpowder flashed, that meant there was sufficient whisky to allow ignition, and thus it was proved . . .

Queen Victoria discovered the subtle and unique contributions of peat smoke, burn water and the soft air of the Scottish climate during sojourns at her beloved Balmoral, and, in her later days, the monarch unwittingly promoted the sales of Scotland's bottled drams when it became known that she did indeed enjoy a dram in her afternoon tea.

This variation of a hot toddy, which should always be stirred with a silver spoon, is but one offering from the whisky cocktail menu. Another is Atholl Brose, the construction of which requires the following exercise. You mix half a pound of fine oatmeal with a little cold water from the burn for a few minutes. Then you press this plain little mixture through a sieve after half an hour or so; thereafter add half a pound of pure clear heather honey. Then add two pints of whisky (malt or otherwise, according to taste) and stir until frothy. Bottle the mixture, cork it and store it in a cool, dark place for two whole days. Then it will be wonderful.

A Bannockburn cocktail consists of the following ingredients, shaken together violently with crushed ice: a slice of lemon, a dash of Worcester sauce, a single measure of whisky and half a glass of good quality tomato juice, which to a true Scotsman represents English blood (and he knows why).

Arrangements have long been made in Scotland for dear dead and departed souls to continue their intake of the wee dram. During the legal minimum of three years' maturation in the cask, cool clean air steals in through the porous oak, refining and concentrating the contents. This causes some 2 per cent of the whisky to evaporate each year, and this amount is known as 'the angels' share'. In its charity, one large distillery in Dufftown each year loses about 28,000 litres of the stuff. Not 'the clouds of unknowing'.

Single malt whiskies, made from malted barley at one distillery, are the *grands crus* of Scotch whiskies. Each is slightly different, producing taste and flavour descriptions which vary from 'the aroma of wet sheep' to Derek Cooper's memorable comment on Talisker: it is 'not a drink, it is an interior explosion, distilled central heating'.

Scotland's smallest whisky distillery is The Edradour, on Moulin moor north-east of Pitlochry. Selected local barley is malted and dried over peat fires. After the milling it is soaked in soft spring water from the moor in the Mash Tun. The resulting 'wort',

acquiring its bronzed straw colour, is slowly cooled in a Morton refrigerator (the last one operating in Scotland). Fermentation in pine washbacks follows, and yeast is added. The wash is distilled, in the smallest copper stills allowed under excise regulations, at about 180°F, then redistilled, with the experienced stillman retaining only the middle third of the run. About 150 gallons of this spirit are made each week, and stored to mature for about ten years in Oloroso sherry butts beside the village burn. It is a mysterious process, and about as difficult to explain as the lore of cricket to a non-Englishman.

The most northerly whisky distillery is Highland Park, founded in 1826 outside Kirkwall in the Orkneys; it employs spring water which never sees daylight. Scotland's highest is Dalwhinnie, midway between Perth and Inverness. The name means 'the meeting place' in Gaelic, and it was here that in the old days the Highland drovers halted on their way down to the cattle markets in Crieff and Falkirk. 'The Gentle Spirit' is made with the snow-fed waters of the *Allt an t'Sluic* spring from nearby granite rocks. They are one source of the River Spey, along which the great 70-mile Speyside Malt Whisky Trail wends its way and where

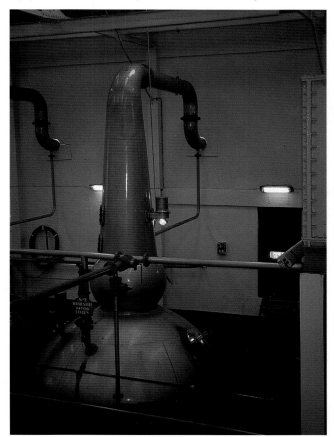

Wash still No. 2 in the Talisker malt whisky distillery on Skye.

The old kitchens at Cawdor Castle.

the wash in the distilling process is called 'Jo'. No one can remember why.

The Lonach Highland and Friendly Society was founded by Sir George Forbes in 1823 to mark his son's coming-of-age, and outrageous games were held on the banks of the River Don, some 20 miles from Braemar. For the occasion Forbes raised the little-known Lonach Highlanders, and 30 years later they paraded their colours before Queen Victoria at Braemar. This, remember, is the person who took a dram of whisky in her afternoon tea as a warm-up for her habitual evening cocktail, which consisted of half a tumbler of single malt whisky topped up with a decent claret. She lived to be 82, and ruled very well.

Most years nowadays there is still a Forbes leading a march of the men of Lonach, in full Highland dress, to Braemar to the sound of pipes and drums. Sometimes they are joined by the Atholl Highlanders, the last Duke of Atholl's private army (the only one in Europe), with bayonets fixed. Many are the stops taken along the way, via Strathdon, and on the way back as well. The number of sustaining drams, taken of vital necessity, annually becomes a legend within its own day.

Whisky galore, then, and also the title of Compton Mackenzie's celebrated novel, published in 1947. It fictionalises the wonderfully true story of how SS *Politician* foundered on the rocks of South Uist in 1942. Her cargo included 20,000 cases of whisky, to which the islanders reluctantly addressed themselves. It is said that thousands of bottles remain buried on the island, so you will need to know that the location for the successful film of the incident was on Eiriosgaigh in the Sound of Barra.

The boom period for whisky for Scotland was definitely the 1890s, when 33 new distilleries were opened. Two thirds of these were along Speyside. By the end of the century there were 161 distilleries pouring out Scotch whisky. There are now fewer than a hundred. This coincided with the devastating spread of phylloxera through the vineyards of France and Europe which, as I have said, affected the quality of brandy as well as wine. Whisky and its blends therefore came into their own.

A dram of whisky is traditionally not wee at all when taken privately, but about half a tumbler, and the procedure for addressing oneself to it in the morning is as follows. The first draught is taken upon awakening, the second while resting on the elbow, the third just before leaving the bed, the fourth before the putting on of the socks, and the fifth while cleaning the teeth. This gives a good start to the day.

In about 1884 a member of the House of Lords, who perhaps commenced his day in this fashion, was thus encouraged to stand up and seriously propose that whisky should be freely available to all the population for health purposes.

Why is Dunvegan Castle portrayed on The Wine Society's Special Highland Whisky label? The answer is that The Wine Society's very first chairman, from 1874 until 1895, was the MacLeod of MacLeod, the 25th chief. From the sixteenth century onwards, whisky gradually overtook ale as the most popular beverage. Centuries ago, whisky was of course drunk at breakfast, and a quart a day was a normal level of consumption. Drinking tumblers were made of staved wood. A bicker was a small stone drinking vessel which sometimes had a glass bottom, so that you could watch out. Loyal toasts were handed round the table in quaichs, round shallow drinking bowls normally carved or turned in wood; horn and silver versions were also traditional. These larger ones had four handles or lugs and were passed from hand to hand.

About another kind of dram. The Gaelic expression *an dram buidheach* means 'the dram that satisfies', and lends its name to one of Scotland's oldest liqueurs. The story of Drambuie has both sad and happy aspects. When Bonnie Prince Charlie fled to the Western Isles, after his army's defeat at Culloden in 1746, the Mackinnons of Strathaird on Skye took him in. In gratitude the Prince, having no other gift to offer in thanks, passed on his secret whisky-based recipe for the liqueur. A Mackinnon still prepares the essence in privacy to this day.

When James VI of Scotland became James I of England in 1603 he immediately ordered that the heraldic red lion of Scotland should be displayed on all public buildings, and this is why there are well over 600 pubs in England and Scotland with a red lion sign hanging outside.

Heather ale (*Leannfraoch*) is once again being made in Scotland, and delicious it is (with a serving of clootie dumplings). R.L. Stevenson wrote of it:

> From the bonny bells of heather,
> They brewed a drink long syne,
> Was sweeter far than honey,
> Was stronger far than wine.

Arbroath was once one of Scotland's great fishing ports.

The earliest brewers among the one or two oldest distilleries in Great Britain were Benedictine monks from the Isle of May in the Firth of Forth. They were granted holdings on the mainland and dug wells in 1415 to find water ideally suited to the brewing of beer. After secularisation in the 1500s, beer came from that brewery for the Scottish-French Expeditionary Force which was garrisoned for a time at Dunbar Castle. The present brewery was under construction in 1719, and James Boswell wrote of its brew: 'the best small beer I ever had'. A little more than a hundred years later the Emperor of Austria proclaimed that he kept a Scotch ale in his cellar and termed it 'the Burgundy of Scotland'.

Another excellent draught is Traquair House ale, which is brewed under the direction of this wonderful old house's owner, Catherine Maxwell Stuart, the 21st laird of Traquair. Brewing at Traquair starts early. In the oak tun roasted barley and pale malt are infused with local spring water. Then they are boiled with hops from east Kent over a gas flame in an open brew kettle of copper which is dated 1739. There follow three days of fermentation, and then three months of maturation in metal casks.

Beer was involved in the construction of Traquair House's famous Bear Gates. They are at the end of a quarter-of-a-mile-long avenue leading to the house, and have now been closed for more than 250 years.

Prince Charles Edward Stuart was the last person to pass through the gates, and he had arrived to encourage support for his cause to get the Stuarts back on to the throne. The fifth Earl of Traquair closed the gates and issued a solemn promise that they would never again be opened until the Stuarts were restored. The Maxwell Stuart records show that the Bear Gate pillars cost £12 15s to build, the two bears on top of each cost £10 4s, and the workmen were rewarded with four gallons of the ale to encourage their erection of the gates.

Now, there is a famous recipe for the perfect Scotch breakfast; it consists of a bottle of whisky, a haggis and a collie dog. Why, you may ask, the collie dog? The answer, of course, is to eat the haggis.

☆ ★ ☆ ★ ☆ ★ ☆

The renowned 'Arbroath Smokies'. Small, fresh haddock have been split, and are being smoked over burning oak chips at the E. & O. Company in Arbroath.

Haggis is banned from sale in the United States of America. The Federal Food and Drug Administration refuses import licences on account of the fact that one of Scotland's culinary glories is judged to be 'unfit for human consumption'.

American visitors to Scotland think differently of course. Queues form for offal and oatmeal trapped in sheep's stomachs. Haggis soup is a recent arrival, but cocktail 'haggae' crucified on little wooden sticks, and tinned haggis (in skin) have long been available for discerning persons. There is scarcely a thought for the literal fact that, credit to one Owen Griffith, the food is an acronym for Highland Agricultural Gunk Gathered In Stomachs.

Is haggis translatable? Probably not. After all, haggis has been called 'faggot with attitude'. For a Frenchman marooned in Scotland on St Andrew's Day (30 November), the dictionaries in his bags would not help out. Hachette's states that haggis is *panse de brebis farcie*; Robert's ducks the challenge: *plat national écossais*. You won't of course locate tatties and neeps in such works.

What a haggis ('Great chieftain o' the puddin' race!' –

Robert Burns) really is has been neatly and definitively summarised by Alexander Maclean in his notable work *The Haggis* (published by Famedram, PO Box 3, Ellon AB41 9EA). He correctly draws attention to the rutting seasons of the haggis, May and October, when the haggis ranches on Mull are closed to visitors for their own safety. Apparently the Mull haggis is the purest strain, as cross-breeding with mainland animals has been successfully prevented. A Glen More haggis is widely appreciated for its flavour; Alexander Maclean tells us that it eats about three times its own weight in white heather just before sundown each day. The noted lack of white heather in many parts of Scotland is due to the dietary requirements of both wild and domestic haggis.

A golden spurtle, or theevil, is the main prize in the World Porridge-Making Championships held in Carrbridge. Contestants come all the way from the Western Isles, and it is always a stirring occasion. A nice local granny called Florence Ritchie, the only woman finalist, won the honours in the first competition in

E. & O. Company's fish business in Arbroath.

1994; her method was to soak fresh oatmeal overnight, cook with cold local water and a pinch of salt, stir all the while, and add a dash of fresh cream before serving. Simple, like so many Scottish mysteries.

However, Mrs Ritchie failed to use rainwater, a traditional ingredient for purists. Porridge (*brochan*) must always be addressed as 'they', and this plurality should always be stirred clockwise with a spurtle held in the right hand. They (Robert Burns's 'chief of Scotia's food') must always be eaten when standing up. They are correctly taken from a large single bowl which should be made of hard wood, and consumed (after being dunked in individual helpings of buttermilk, cream or cold milk) with a spoon crafted from horn, which does not conduct heat.

The old cooking ranges naturally had baking girdles hanging over open fires. These were first made in Culross in Fife, and for a short period the town actually owned the exclusive rights to their manufacture. Early kitchens included ashets (serving plates, coming from the French *assiettes*), spoons made of horn, which were cleaner than wood (most communities had their own horn workers and their work was often beautifully decorated), and sugar loaf cutters, often called nippers or snippers. There were clockwork bottlejacks; these were eighteenth-century successors to elaborate hot air, water, and sometimes dog-driven spits. They were suspended before open fires with joints hung beneath them, slowly revolving over trays which caught the falling fat. Pewter was widely used for plates. A salt box was ever present — with leather hinges, of course, because salt rusts metal — and there were copper pans which conduct heat so well. These were tinned inside to prevent verdigris, and their outsides were cleaned with lemon skins which had been dipped in salt and silversand. In addition there were always sturdy, three-legged, blackened iron pots which sat on open fires on the ground.

Local blacksmiths were vital to those early kitchens. From their forges came the girdles, fire baskets, toasting racks, pot-chains (or swees), grid irons, cauldrons and spades for the making of the bannocks. Blacksmiths also produced all the basic ironwork for the house. Scottish kitchenalia is so collectable because these items were, by definition, all different. About 300 years ago travelling people (*ceardan*) were important contributors to community services because they were

The oldest extant kitchen in Scotland, at Skara Brae, which is about 5,000 years old. The hearthstones are in the foreground.

the menders of those pots, pans, kettles and so on, and very often worked in horn if there was no local horn worker. They also did other odd jobs, such as cleaning pots, and also the baskets in which bannocks were stored, with heather. They attended to the horn spoons which every man had fastened to his side. Sometimes there was the little whistle at the end of their handles to repair.

There is a fine extant example of a central stone hearth in the famous Black House on the Isle of Lewis, and a visit there immediately demonstrates the atmosphere during a meal taken around such a fire. The museum in Elgin has a fine display of domestic interiors reproduced. Another good example of a smokehouse-type kitchen can be seen in the Highland Folk Museum in Kingussie. The seats around those central fires in the early days had very short legs because the fact was that the clearest area was near the bed of the fire, and so you sat as near as possible to the floor.

The English often claim that kippers were invented in Northumberland. The Scots, on the other hand, claim that they probably originated in Loch Fyne, that long, deep loch. It is probable that both claimants are in error. The word 'küppen', which means 'to spawn', is, in fact, a Dutch word and it was applied to the act of smoking an out-of-season salmon. Once upon a time kippers were known as 'Glasgow Magistrates' on account of the size of their girth. The secret of a good kipper is to have it smoked very slowly, maybe for up to 15 hours, and the best wood shavings to use in the fireboxes are from sherry casks.

Another great treat from the smokehouse is a hot freshly smoked Arbroath smokie, which, scraped out of the skin with your fingers on the spot, is a very special experience indeed.

The Finnan haddock, which is split open, cured and coloured with smoke, is named after the village of Findon, a fishing village north-east of Portlethen, south of Aberdeen. It was in this village that the Findon or Finnan haddock was first cured and smoked. The Scottish Finnan 'haddie' or haddock has its backbone on the right.

Sir Walter Scott wrote four nice lines about the fishermen in the Firth of Forth:

The herring loves the merry moonlight,
The mackerel loves the wind,
But the oyster loves the dredging-song
For he comes of gentle kind.

Molluscs from the Island of Barra, in the Western Isles, are the finest to be had, and their greatest breeding ground is the Traigh Mhor, the big beach which is occasionally an airport. It happens to be Europe's only tidal airport and has been operating since the 1930s. Literally millions of molluscs breed off this enormous beach.

Records of superstitions abound in this book, and many are attached to relationships and marriage. Centuries ago in Galloway, a girl who was looking for a husband would pick some green grass, repeating the rhyme:

New moon, new moon, tell me if you can,
Gif I have a hair like the hair o' my gudman.

She then carefully examined the grass to see if a hair was among it. If so, the colour of it would be the colour of her future husband's.

Sir Walter Scott noted in his *Journal* that James Hogg received a certain Mrs Johnston and offered her a glass of water from a fairy well at Altrive (the place of Hogg's last residence). The great poet said to her, 'Hae ony merrit wummin wha drinks a tumbler o' this will hae twuns in a twalmont.' 'In that case, Mr Hogg,' said Mrs Johnston, 'I shall only take half a tumbler.'

Another encouragement to procreate was a popular ancient aphrodisiac called skate-bree – the water in which skate had been boiled.

Where vegetables are concerned, in Lowland Scotland they were very rarely served in the old days at weddings because they were considered to be unlucky for such an occasion.

In the Outer Hebrides in the old days, on 29 September (St Michael's Day), a cake called 'Struan Micheil' was traditionally baked. It consisted of a mixture of barley, oats and rye and was covered on both sides with generous helpings of butter, cream and eggs. In this respect it resembled the Beltane bannock (from the Gaelic *bonnach*). It has been recorded that 250 years ago Beltane bannocks were summarily treated; each person present in a room faced the fire, broke off a piece of bannock and flung it over his left shoulder,

saying: 'This I give to thee, preserve thou my horses; this to thee, preserve thou my sheep,' and so on. The host then mounted his chair, placed one foot on the dining table and raised up a glass of good cheer in his right hand. His toast went:

Up with it, up with it, up with it!
Down with it, down with it, down with it!
Away from me, away from me, away from me!
Towards me, towards me, towards me!
Drink it off.

He then tossed the glass over his left shoulder and shouted the last line:

And no other shall ever drink from this glass again.

A few words about words. Scots are not too pleased that the word 'scone' comes from *sgonn*, which actually means a 'shapeless mass'. With regard to shortbread, the expression is literal. The Scots used 'bread' to describe an oat biscuit or an oat bread cooked on a bakestone or girdle. It becomes short when you add fat or shortening, which also makes it richer. Incidentally, the pinching around the edges of shortbread recalls rites of ancient sun worship. 'Cakes' – as in oatcakes – recalls the old Scots word 'kaak', which means a 'slice'. And the reason why people who live in the better parts of Scottish cities are called 'pan loafies' is that they were better able to afford a loaf of bread that had an all-over crust, and not just a plain loaf with a crust on the top only.

Potatoes were introduced into the Highlands of Scotland in the 1740s and within 100 years were providing about 80 per cent of the national diet there, replacing oats. ('Which, in England, is generally given to horses, but in Scotland supports people' – Dr Samuel Johnson.) Therefore when a potato blight occurred in those days, as for example in 1845 and also the following year, a terrible famine was always the result.

The meat of the deer has always been a staple part of the Scotsman's diet. Sir Walter Scott, who has recorded so much for us, wrote in *The Lady of the Lake* that during the reign of Edward VI a Frenchman witnessed 'a great hunting party at which a most wonderful quantity of game was destroyed'. He saw these 'Scottish savages' devour a part of their venison raw without any preparation at all other than compressing it between two batons of wood so as to force out the blood and render it extremely hard. These savages reckoned such a 'dish' a great delicacy.

Baxter's famous Royal Game Soup had its origins in 1929 when William Baxter, who was a brilliant salesman, was on one of his selling trips in Upper Speyside. He accidentally tripped over a pile of full sacks on the darkened platform of Aviemore station, and learned from the station master that they contained venison. It occurred to him then and there that there might be some extra potential in the abundance of game which existed on his very doorstep. His redoubtable wife Ethel, who was recorded as having helped make three tons of soup on the night before the birth of their first son Gordon, modified an old family recipe to produce the Royal Game Soup that we know and appreciate today. It was also Ethel who developed cock-a-leekie and Scotch broth. William Baxter's father, George Baxter, had founded the company back in 1868, and he lived in Moray, a rich district in terms of good soil, forest deer and so on. Barter in those days was common, and Baxter's customers often gave him good garden produce in exchange for his goods, and it was the fruit that he so often received which inspired the preparation of jams and jellies in the back of their shop in Fochabers, seven miles east of Elgin.

In Scotland you can still find on the tables in the distant Highlands and elsewhere some of the following diverting concoctions: seaweed soup, sea moss jelly, liver ketchup, deer horn jelly, birch wine, sheep's head broth and calves' foot jelly. More certainly to be found on the breakfast tables is a pot of marmalade, and it will more or less certainly be Keiller's Dundee Orange Marmalade. In the story of its invention it is instructive to remember that the Portuguese for 'quince jelly' is *marmalade*, and the Spanish for 'jam' is *mermelada*. A young Dundee grocer by the name of James Keiller bought up an entire consignment of bitter Seville oranges down at the docks in Dundee in the cold winter of 1700 – but nobody would buy them from him. So his wife substituted the Seville oranges for quinces, which were an ingredient in one of her old family recipes, and thus the famous Dundee marmalade was born.

Cattle thieving in Scotland used to be a very frequent event, because a head of cattle was in fact a currency unit. Thus they were protected by tradition, and stories have come down about them. Thomas Pennant wrote:

In some parts of the country is a rural sacrifice on Mayday. A cross is cut on some sticks which are dipped in potage and on the Thursday before Easter one of each was placed over the sheep-cot, the stable and the cow-house. On the first of May they are carried to the hill, where the rites are celebrated, all decked with wild flowers, and after the feast is over, replaced over the spots where they were taken from.

On 2 May in many parts of Scotland, honeysuckle was placed in cowsheds to prevent the cattle within being influenced by the causes of witches.

In the last century on the Island of Coll in the Western Isles, the sign of a cross was made in salt on the back of a cow when it was calving. The same holy rite was performed on the pail containing the first milk obtained from a cow.

Two hundred or more years ago in Aberdeenshire, it was widely believed that flint arrowheads exposed by weather and plough in the fields had been fired at livestock by evil fairies. If an elfshot was found near a cow or a horse, suspicion was aroused and the vet had to be sent for – and naturally did nothing to discourage such a profitable superstition.

Food often had a part to play in Beltane rites in the olden days in the Highlands. Near Kingussie, hardboiled eggs and bannocks were rolled down the hills on 1 May, and they had a purpose to play in the role of divination. On one side of each was marked a cross and on the other a circle. The bannocks were rolled down three times and the owner of each had to witness which of the signs turned up most often when the bannock came to rest at the foot of the hill. The cross, of course, represented life, and the circle death.

Special cakes were baked for the ancient Gaelic festival of Samhuinn, nowadays known as Hallowe'en, celebrated on the eve of All Saints' Day. These were to ward off evil spirits and nasty superstitions and to welcome good fortune. The Hallowe'en cake was always prepared with charms; if you found a button you would have a singular pleasure of your own choosing, a horseshoe meant good luck, and a ring meant that you would marry shortly. The discovery of a coin in a dish of cream and oatmeal foretold marriage for its finder; these traditions are carried on all over the country to this day with the inclusion of charms and coins in Christmas puddings.

Until quite recently, Hogmanay was regarded in Scotland as being far more important than Christmas.

As recently as the 1960s, Christmas was not even a public holiday north of the border, with shops, offices and pubs open as usual until 30 December, when Hogmanay began. The word comes from an old French word *Hoguinané*. Hogmanay is a time for haggis, bashed tatties and neeps, first footing, black bun (fruit cake), Het Pint for 'first fits', and skirling to bagpipes. Doors are, alas, no longer left open to let the spirit of the Auld Year slip away. This day has been celebrated for over 200 years in Kirkwall, Orkney Islands, with Boys' and Men's Ba' Games, starting with a ba' thrown down from the Mercat Cross. Goals for the Uppies and the Doonies, respectively, are the site of an old castle and the harbour.

Burns Night suppers are held each year on 25 January, with Scots and their friends getting together for an evening of entertainment to celebrate the birth of the late, great Ayrshire poet. Traditionally it starts with Scottish country dancing and recitations of some of Burns's poems. The performances should always include 'Tam o' Shanter' and the 'Address to the Unco Guid'. Haggis, bashed tatties and neeps are once again served and, after a lone or collective recitation of 'To a Haggis', that revered dish is often piped into the dining room on grand occasions, and the first cut of it is made with the skean-dhu, the small knife that Scotsmen wear on formal occasions.

Burns Night suppers end with a lusty rendition of 'Auld Lang Syne'. Much the same behaviour accompanies activities on St Andrew's Night on 30 November, the feast day of the first-century Galilean apostle who is Scotland's patron saint. Nowadays only three verses are sung of 'Auld Lang Syne', which was first published at the end of the seventeenth century, and probably not originally written by Robert Burns. They are the first verse, the chorus and the last verse. It is quite wrong to sing the first verse with arms crossed. Only when the last verse starts with the words 'and there's a hand my trusty fiere' are hands released, arms crossed and hands thereafter reclasped. And only when the second verse, which is the chorus, commences should everybody walk repeatedly to the middle of the floor, and back again.

It was Prince Albert, according to Queen Victoria's diaries, who said: 'Things taste better in small houses.' And she went on to record that she did indeed enjoy what she called 'the celebrated haggis'. Queen Victoria enjoyed all of the pleasures outlined in this chapter, and nowhere more than in what she called 'a small Cottage' in Dunkeld, of which a close friend of hers had the use. Perhaps before indulging they intoned a famous grace (which the author's own grandmother always retailed before every meal). It is called 'The Selkirk Grace', and is yet another set of words attributed to Robert Burns:

Some hae meat, and canna eat,
And some wad eat that want it;
But we hae meat and we can eat,
And sae the Lord be thankit.

Chapter Eight

ISLAND MYSTERIES

Aonghais, Bottle Island, Carn Deas, Carn Iar, Eilean a'Chleirich, Eilean Dubh, Eilean Mullagrach, Glas-leac Beag, Glas-leac Mor, Horse Island, Isle Ristol, Tanera Beag, Tanera Mor . . . The euphony of these Summer Isles conjures up a kind of siren song. You feel that one day you must answer the call, and take the ferry over. Then you can post a letter in the smallest stamp-issuing 'country' in the world, and share the secrets of these north-western islands.

And so it is with many of Scotland's beautiful islands; they sound alluring and all have unique and significant pasts. An island is held to be solid land, surrounded by water, with sufficient vegetation to support one or more sheep, or which is inhabited by man. By this definition there are 787 in Scotland, and many are grouped in distinct archipelagos. About 160 of them make up the Inner and Outer Hebrides, and 152 are distributed in the Orkneys and Shetlands.

Today many of these are uninhabited. Most of the rest are not in formally named groups. In the Firth of Forth, off the east coast, can be found Bass Rock, Craigleith, Cramond, Fidra, Inchcolm, Inchgarrie, Inchkeith, Inchmickery (Inch-, from the Gaelic *innis*, 'island'), Isle of May and Lamb. To the south-west lie Ailsa Craig, Arran, Bute, Devar, Great Cumbrae, Holy Isle, Little Cumbrae, Pladda and Sanda. All with tales to tell.

Alegend tells of how the **Orkney Islands** came into being. There was once a sea dragon called the Stoor Worm which lived off the northern coast of Scotland. He would only behave if he had regular offerings of seven virgins, in a batch, which were to be left for him each Saturday, bound hand and foot, on the seashore. One day the dragon was killed when a young man rowed a boat into his body and set fire to his liver. He rose up out of the sea, and as he died his tongue flew out and came to constitute the Baltic Sea. With a great roar his teeth then fell out; some made up the Orkney Islands and more the Shetlands. In the end he bound himself up into a huge tight ball and crashed

into the sea, and they say that Iceland is his body, with the liver still burning beneath the sea.

The fact is that the 'Orcades' were first mentioned by the Greek voyager Pytheas in about 300 BC. He referred to the Britons as *Prettanoi*, which is ancient Greek for the Celtic word *Pritani*, which meant 'the painted ones'. From *Pritani* comes the Latin word *Britannia* ('Land of the Britanni') and so also, of course, 'Britain'. The reference to the painted ones has much relevance to the most remarkable Neolithic settlement of Skara Brae on Mainland in the Orkney Islands. It is very well preserved because it was covered by sand for over 5,000 years, until a terrible storm one night in 1850 in the Bay of Skaill tore aside the topsoil to reveal this set of 'houses'. During the excavations that followed there were found among the domestic 'houseware' dishes containing traces of blue, red and yellow pigments and it is thought that these were used by the natives to adorn themselves. (A painted Scotsman is still a fearsome sight today at Murrayfield or Hampden Park!)

Neolithic villages such as Skara Brae perhaps housed the astronomer-priests of the day; they were of a privileged order whose job it was to keep an eye on the heavens in order to predict the terrifying occurrence of an eclipse and to maintain a constant watch on the 18.6-year cycle of the moon.

A Neolithic monument of a different class is called the Stones of Stenness, which is a ring going back to 2970 BC. These lovely stones are to be found about 4 miles east of Stromness, and only four of them are left standing in this 104-foot circle. Originally 12 of the stones had most distinct slanted tops, with each at a different angle; the tallest remaining one stands 16 feet 6 inches above the ground (there will be another third of that height beneath). The mystery of their purpose may never be solved, but it has been proposed that they were once part of a huge astronomical observatory, with Britons stationed constantly to look up along the smooth angles of sight in order to note diurnal movements in the night sky. A village-type settlement rather similar to Skara Brae has been discovered very recently very near the Stones of Stenness.

The ruins of the Abbot's House, near the Abbey on Iona.

The most complete ring of stones in the Orkneys is also on Mainland and is known as the Ring of Brodgar. The late Professor Thom, the Scots surveyor, believed that it was a prehistoric observatory, with its 60 stones set very precisely around an elliptical (not circular) shape. Four of the stones bear different carvings – an anvil, a cross, an ogham and a runic inscription – and it is almost certain that we will never know what they 'said'.

That runic inscription may have been added in about the twelfth century when Vikings broke into the other great and impressive monument in the Orkney Islands, that of Maes Howe. This huge and beautifully constructed chambered cairn, which is covered by a mound 24 feet high, has fabulously dressed stones inside. The Vikings left behind them 24 runic inscriptions and also pictorial carvings, including a marvellous one of a dragon (perhaps a reminder of that dragon legend mentioned above?). They also made reference to buried treasure but none has been found so far.

The **Shetland Islands** are closer to Iceland than London. They share the same latitude as St Petersburg in Russia and Cape Farewell in Greenland, which means cold, dark winters and no nights in the middle of summer. This did not deter Harald the Fairheaded of Norway from sailing over and chasing the Vikings out of the islands, which were until then known as *Inse Katt* ('Cat Islands'). Norway ruled the Shetlands from 911 until 1468, which was the year when a highly satisfactory plan went awry. James III of Scotland married Margaret, daughter of Christian I of the combined kingdoms of Denmark and Norway. The King was unable to produce most of the agreed dowry, and so he had to forfeit all his rights and property in the islands.

The Vikings and Norsemen were by no means the first inhabitants of the Shetlands. The archaeological site at Jarlshof, on Mainland, derives its name from that of the laird's house in Sir Walter Scott's *The Pirate*. It is not apparent why this area, on the eastern shore of the west Voe of Sumburgh, should have been chosen over 3,500 years ago as the location for wheelhouses, a broch, a domestic settlement (between 2000 and 1000 BC) and later a Viking 'village'.

The 43-foot-high broch on **Mousa**, a small island

This standing stone on Mull was no doubt in place before the stone walling arrived.

off Mainland, is one of the finest and most complete in Scotland. A stairway inside winds upwards through the six surviving galleries inside. It was probably a kind of barracks.

The island of **Foula**, 27 miles west of Scalloway in the Shetland Islands, can fairly lay claim to be one of Britain's loneliest yet loveliest islands. One of its unusual aspects is that it is one of the very last places in Europe which observes the festival of Christmas according to the old Julian calendar, on 6 January. The rest of us changed to the Gregorian way of reckoning dates back in 1752. Realistically one suspects that the traditional Christmas is preceded by a modest celebration of the Gregorian one, so that there is just one long celebration. Most European countries changed their calendars in 1582, and the rest of Scotland moved the first day of its year from 25 March to 1 January in 1600. Russia switched as late as 1918, and so the still-inhabited island of Foula is a unique remnant of the old calendar.

'The Long Island' was, until this century, the name of Britain's only island with two names: **Lewis** and **Harris**. Its westerly and remote neighbour St Kilda can

incidentally compete in the oddity stakes; it is the only one named after a saint who has never existed.

The world-famous Harris Tweed is in reality Lewis Tweed, but the name stays, as it was first manufactured in Harris and is still shipped through Tarbert on Harris. The Harris Tweed Authority (founded in 1909) awards its ancient and distinctive 'Orb Mark' to wool products which have been made from 100 per cent pure virgin wool, dyed, spun and finished in the Outer Hebrides, and hand-woven by islanders in their own homes on their looms 'in the islands of Lewis, Harris, Uist, Barra and their several purtenances'. 'Tweed' is a 150-year-old misspelling of 'tweel', as in twill.

Scotland's weather patterns have always ordained the need for tough outer clothing. Before the arrival of automated factory methods about 100 years ago, the shrinking of cloth on these islands was naturally undertaken by teams of women (never men). After freshly woven cloth had been soaked in hot, stale human urine, it was sewn into a circle and spread out on a table. A row of women sat each side of this table and kneaded the cloth as it passed before them. This

Black House No. 42 at Arnol on Lewis, which was occupied until 1964. Livestock was kept inside on the right in the winter months, while the living quarters in this single-storeyed earth-floored building were on the left.

centuries-old activity was accompanied by 'waulking songs' (*òrcin lunadhaidh*) in which the working women recalled ancient stories, legends and historical facts from all over the Highlands and islands. Records of some of them are the sole repositories of long-forgotten Scottish beliefs, customs and practices.

A great storm in Lewis in the winter of 1831 left exposed on the beach at Uig, on the west coast, 67 chessmen made from walrus tusk. It was later proved that the four-inch-high pieces were made in Scandinavia or Iceland between 1150 and 1175 and are the finest surviving medieval chesspieces. 'The Lewis chessmen' came from six game sets, but unfortunately none was complete.

The farmer whose cow is supposed to have stumbled on them fled from the beach, believing that the gloomy faces on the pieces represented demonic spirits. They were soon sold for £85, they left Lewis, and 11 of them are now in the National Museum of Scotland, while the remaining 56 reside in the British Museum. Echoes here of the Elgin marbles situation . . . but, then again, they did not originate from Lewis.

Fourteen miles west of Stornoway, the 'Long Island's' capital, stand the most exciting and mysterious set of standing stones in Scotland. They are on a prominent, high, sloping site outside Callanish, and are often called 'the Stonehenge of the North'. Dating from about 1800 BC, they consist of an ellipse of 13 tall, slim, undressed stones, and another (the tallest at 15 feet six inches) in their centre. Four unfinished avenues of single rows of stones lead away to the east, south and west, and there is a double row just east of north. The grand central stone is to the west of a later chamber tomb. So what exactly was this amazing piece of prehistoric engineering for? The most popular answer is that it was another 'lunar observatory'. And yet its local name is *Tursachan*, which means 'a place of pilgrimage or mourning'.

The great man-made glory of Harris is the church dedicated to St Clement at Rodel at the southern end of the island (already mentioned in chapter two). Many of the early MacLeods of Dunvegan and Harris were buried there. The last resting place of Alexander (Alasdair Crotach, 'the humpback'), chief of the clan, was exquisitely carved and constructed a full 20 years before he died. On the tower of the church, which is dedicated to the pious memory of a first-century Pope, is a *sheila-na-gig* — a carving of a naked lady in a squatting position with her knees wide apart. Pre-Reformation evil spirits must have been involved in

The reality of life inside the Black House at Arnol, Lewis. These centuries-old dwellings are so called because of their smoke-blackened interiors.

her conception – but to attract them or ward them off?

In one of his *Songs of Travel*, Robert Louis Stevenson included this wistful verse:

> Sing me a song of a lad that is gone,
> Say, could that lad be I?
> Merry of soul he sailed on a day
> Over the sea to Skye.

Today Stevenson would have to walk or motor across a 100,000-ton concrete bridge to Skye, and then he would doubtless sit himself down and scribble a characteristic obituary for long-cherished views from the Kyle of Lochalsh over the sea towards the forbidding Cuillin hills, ever-garlanded in roving mists, and *Eilean Bàn*, where stands the derelict cottage of Gavin Maxwell (the author of the bestseller *Ring of Bright Water*).

'Skye' in Old Norse means 'island of the mists', and obviously the weather has not noticeably improved. The Black and Red Hills of the Cuillins form perhaps the most spectacular range of mountains in Great Britain. They are visible from everywhere on the island, and their aloof splendour has always inspired local legends. An Irish giant long ago came to do battle; he strode ashore at Talisker, and fought for two days and a night in the Cuillins before he finally triumphed against an unknown adversary. To this day, some islanders still call the range The Cuchullins, after him.

The Whalebone Arch on the west coast of Lewis. It consists of the jawbones of a blue whale which came ashore in 1920.

A family shearing session on Lewis. All Harris Tweed is in fact produced on Lewis.

The italicised Gaelic words throughout this book are there in recognition of the fact that there is an ever-growing interest in the language and its ancient culture. Once upon a time the Hebrides, and particularly Skye and Iona, were homes to centres of important cultures on a European level. On Skye there is a Gaelic college, *Sabhal Mor Ostaig*, which has plans to develop itself into a college campus with international links, a visitors' centre and so on, on the east coast of Sleat, in the south. It is a fact that some 70 per cent of local children now either speak or write Gaelic. All public information signs are in two languages.

The MacLeods, MacDonalds and Mackinnons have made full contributions to the lore and legends of Skye. The Bloody Stone, near Harta Corrie, commemorates the scene of a bloody battle between the first two of these clans, and great numbers of kilted soldiers are still occasionally sensed to be in the vicinity. Believe it or not, a driverless 1934 Austin motor car is often seen roaring along some of Skye's remoter roads and trackways.

John MacLeod of MacLeod, the present clan chief, has his home in huge, romantic Dunvegan Castle in the north-west, on the loch of that name with its seal island. He told me a remarkable and true story. Five years ago he received a letter from a civil engineer by the name of MacLeod who lived in Oregon. In it he asked the clan chief if he could visit Dunvegan, because it would be the conclusion of an important personal mission.

This is how you catch the ferry from Oskamull on Mull to the small island of Ulva.

The abbey on Iona. It is always a tranquil place because the great numbers of visitors have such respect for it.

This bookcase was the gift of the travel agent Thomas Cook to the people of Iona in 1845.

When he arrived he told his tale. The ghost of a MacLeod ancestor of his was confined to a leather washbag which he kept in a cupboard upstairs in his Oregon home. It had started to complain that it no longer cared for the materialism of contemporary American life, and wished to return to the land of his fathers – Skye, and Dunvegan. The engineer produced a very ordinary-looking, fawn-coloured, rectangular washbag, which was, unusually, padlocked, and handed it and the keys to John MacLeod, with tears of gratitude and relief in his eyes. He asked him to allow the ghost to settle back into his ways, and not to unlock the washbag for a year or two.

And so the washbag resided on top of a cupboard in Dunvegan Castle's dining room for three years and more, until, one Christmas Day, the clan chief and his family decided that the time had come to unlock the washbag. Inside rested a faded bonnet in a tartan which was not that of the MacLeods. That is the end of a strange but true story.

Dunvegan Castle, claimed sometimes to be the oldest castle in Britain to be built by the family which still inhabits it, is possessor of, and guarded by, its Fairy Flag. The eight-square-foot silk flag has many legends attached to it. One says that if it is produced in battle, the MacLeods' enemies believe they are facing more men than they are – but it can only be waved three times.

The basaltic island of **Canna** is south of Skye and the Cuillin Sound, and north-west of Rhum. Occupied now by just a few families and in the stewardship of the National Trust for Scotland, this island used to have, 150 years ago, a population of about 450 people. Recent excavations have revealed that there was once a chapel dedicated to St Columba, that great Scottish ecclesiastical hero, on this small island, very near a Celtic cross. Looking at the shape of the island it is easy to believe that the origin of its name is the Gaelic word for 'young whale', leaping about as it does from west to east. St Columba's biographer, Adamnan, in his biography of St Columba, *Vita Sancti Columbae*, which he completed in about AD 695, makes mention six times of an island, hitherto unidentified, called either Himba or Hinba. It is now believed that these references must surely represent Canna, home to one of the most important early Christian buildings in Scotland.

A hill in the north-west of Canna is known as Compass Hill, because of its violent and unnatural effect on magnetic needles.

Eigg, three miles north-east of Muck and four miles south-east of Rhum, takes its name from *ec*, meaning 'hollow' or 'nick', which refers to the glen which intersects the 24-square-mile island across its middle. A deep, narrow cave in the south was once the scene of a terrible massacre. More than 200 MacDonalds, with their wives and children, took refuge within it at the end of the sixteenth century, to escape from invading MacLeods. After two days they were discovered and a great fire was lit at its mouth. They were all put to death by suffocation.

Mull from the air has the appearance of a crayfish, or even a kind of squashed Britain, or so it occurred to me within the comfort of one of Scotland's longest-established still-family-owned hotels: the Mishnish on the harbour front in Tobermory. A fine handmade map of this, the third largest Hebridean island, hangs inside a sturdy doorway which is built to withstand the constant gale-force winds and driving rain.

Bounty hunters familiar with the story of 'The Tobermory Galleon' will have been visitors to this old inn. She lies nearby at the bottom of the sea in the following circumstances.

The small Romanesque chapel next to the abbey on Iona.

For many years, 'The Tobermory Galleon' was believed to be *The Admiral of Florence*, popularly known as the *Florencia*, and as such was supposedly a treasure-ship carrying large sums of money. It has now been established that she was a substantial merchant ship with a crew of about 50 men from the city state of Ragusa (now Dubrovnik), named *Santa Maria della Grazia e San Giovanni Battista*, and that her captain was Luka Ivanoff Kinkovic. She was commandeered in 1586 in Sicily by the Spanish. Three hundred Sicilian troops under the command of Don Diego Tellez Enriquez were put on board and she sailed to Lisbon to join the Spanish Armada, being assembled there for Philip II's proposed invasion of England. Placed in the Levantine Squadron, she was from then on referred to as the *San Juan de Sicilia*.

In September 1588, the much-damaged ship, a straggler from the defeated and dispersed Spanish Armada, anchored in Tobermory Bay. Two months later she sank after a large explosion on board, with much loss of life. Rumours soon grew of great treasure in her holds and this led to many salvage attempts, the latest of which was in the summer of 1982. However, little beyond cannons and coins has been found, and certainly no treasure has been discovered . . . though yet may be.

On Mull there are 13 standing stones, 14 irregular stone settings and one stone circle, Lochbui, below Ben Buie, near the east coast. The Bronze Age ring was first reported and depicted in 1699 by the archaeologist, Celtic scholar and naturalist Edward Lhwyd (1660-1709). In the following year he wrote to a friend, referring to the damp remoteness and quaint customs of Mull: 'One half of my time since I left you has been spent in places quite remote from all correspondence amongst the Hebrides and other Highlands of Scotland, with whom their neighbours seem to have less commerce than they have with either of the Indies.'

The simple and beautifully located church at Torloisk, Kilninian, is the only one in the Western Highlands and islands dedicated to St Ninian. This fifth-century saint was based at Whithorn, in Dumfries and Galloway, in his Candida Casa, a theological foundation of lasting influence.

In the graveyard there are some richly carved monuments, many of them to MacLeans, ancestors of the Compton family of Northampton who still have the land around. One of them was Margaret MacLean Clephane, wife of the second Marquis of Northampton, great, great grandfather of the present Marquis of Northampton.

He has passed to me from family archives this touching story, recorded by his great, great grandmother, of the passing of Lachlan Mor of Duart. Castle Duart is on the south-east coast of Mull, opposite Oban, and still belongs to the head of the clan:

Like Alexander the Great, he was finished at a drinking match, by treachery, by MacLeod of Dunvegan. His body was brought from Aros, his principal castle, to this place (Torloisk) and lay a considerable time in state; after which, it was carried in his war-galley, to the burying place at Iona, where it was interred with military honours. The lament, sung by his vassals and followers, keeping time with their voices, to the long stroke of the war-galley oars, has been handed down through several generations, and is now securely preserved in my music-book. Its name is Carraig-nan-Aros, the strife of Aros. I think it is the finest piece of our Celtic music I ever heard.

The neighbouring island of **Ulva** (from the Viking *Ullfur*, Wolf Island) is famed for a cave where the parents and grandparents of the explorer David Livingstone lived in 1779 while waiting for a croft to become available. The cave had been inhabited as far back as 5650 BC. The Clearances in 1851 left only 150 people on the island, and the MacDonald lairds adopted the habit of demanding a sheep from every newly married tenant; this was an improvement upon a not-uncommon assumption of lairds in those parts that they spent the wedding night with the bride.

There is no evidence that the Picts were ever on **Iona**, but certainly it was inhabited by Dalriadic tribesmen from Ireland in about the fifth century. The Gaelic *Dàl Riata* tribe, from the coastal parts of present-day County Antrim, were to dominate Scotland three and a half centuries later. In his biography of St Columba, Adamnan called the island 'Ioua insula', and today's Iona comes from a misspelling of the 'u'. The story of St Columba and his great role in early Scottish history is given in my introduction.

This is another terrible story from the Marquis of Northampton's archives. 'Revenge', wrote Francis Bacon, 'is a kind of wild justice.'

After the battle of Kilconan, in the Island of Isla [Islay], where one of our greatest Chiefs was kill'd, the field of battle was left quite solitary: the enemy retreated to a considerable distance, leaving the dead unburied; among the slain lay the body of Lachlan, the

The mortarless drystone broch of Dun Carloway, on the west coast of Lewis, is one of Scotland's finest.

The Old Man of Hoy in Orkney, which presents a challenge even to the most experienced mountaineers.

Chief, surrounded by heaps of his followers: 240 of his own name, all gentlemen of noble birth, lay around him, besides his peasantry, and private followers: a widow, who was a MacLean, settled in Isla, came to search among the slain, for the body of her Chief, which, with those of his gentlemen, had been left, as they fell, within the water-mark, on the sand. She brought with her, her servant, a lad of the opposite clan, MacDonald, and her little car, to carry the body away. She placed it on the car, and ask'd the lad in Gaelic, whether he would guide the horse to the Church of Kilconan, or support the corpse of her darling? The lad, who, so far from sharing in her sorrow, rather rejoiced in the victory obtained by his clan, replied, he would lead the horse. She endeavour'd to support the body, but the task of keeping it steady went beyond her strength; the inhuman servant turn'd round and laughed at her exertions, and at the degraded situation of the chief's remains. She did not seem to observe this piece of disrespect, but busied herself as before, and when come to the Church, she dug a grave, with the servant's assistance, in the consecrated ground. The chief, roll'd in his tartans, was laid in it, and covered with earth. 'Now,' said the widow, 'lay down the sod'; the servant stoop'd to do so: she drew a dagger, and stabbed him through and through: the stroke was mortal, and as she drew the dagger from the wound, she exclaim'd, 'You shall laugh at my darling no more!' The Church of Kilconan is now in ruins, but the grave of Lachlan Mor is still shewn there.

In 1899, the eighth Duke of Argyll gave sacred sites on the island to the Iona Abbey trustees for them to hold for all time for the nation. These were the roofless abbey, the ruined remains of a nunnery and the ancient burial ground of countless kings and chieftains, the *Reilig Orain*.

The abbey church was restored between 1902 and 1910 by public subscription and is, unusually, available for worship by any branch of the Christian church. Later the Iona community was founded by Lord MacLeod of Fuinary, and the monastic buildings were rebuilt between 1938 and 1967 under his leadership.

The marble effigies in Iona Abbey are of the eighth Duke of Argyll (1823–1900) with his wife.

There has been a library on Iona since 1820, when a visiting minister, the Reverend Legh Richmond, raised money to present books. Other benefactors made similar contributions over the years and the books were housed in the school. In 1904, a library building, funded by the Scottish philanthropist Andrew Carnegie, was opened on the island.

The *Oban Times* of 22 August 1885 reported that on the evening of 12 August, a large number of islanders, children and visitors gathered in the island's school to receive a bookcase filled with books from a Mr Thomas Cook. From 1847, Cook had been running rail and steamer excursions to the Highlands and islands. He regularly accompanied the tours in person, and took a great interest in Iona and its people. Collections he organised had already helped buy books, and also boats and nets for local fishermen. 'The full story of Mr Cook's goodness to Iona would be a lengthy though interesting chapter,' said John MacDonald, Vice-President of the Library Committee, in 1885.

Staffa was formed during the tertiary period of volcanic activity about 65 million years ago, and the island, like the Giant's Causeway in Northern Ireland, remains a detached fragment of the lava flows. Later sea intrusion formed the island and wave action the caves. The column, now basalt, was formed as a result of slow cooling of the lava. Shrinking as it cooled from the top, it cracked into hexagons like drying mud. The cracks followed down through the cooling lava, forming columns. These followed any curves or bends caused in relation to the neighbouring rock mass. Staffa is indeed a daunting place to visit. In about 1824, a guidebook wrote of it 'how you will be wetted and wearied and delayed and frightened and starved and cheated and disappointed and drowned'.

Queen Victoria visited the uninhabited island of Staffa (then known as 'The Boat Cave') in 1847 with her family, so famous had it become. Local boatmen back in 1799 were offering to take travellers to Staffa for 15 shillings and two bottles of whisky!

Of one inn in Tobermory on the harbourside, now called Main Street, the following note was made in 1825: 'The house, its inhabitants, the utensils, the linen and the food were filthy in the extreme, the bedroom had an earth floor and until 11 at night was occupied by drunken fishermen. Wakened at 5 a.m. by a piper.' This was a report on an inn which opened soon after 1787, when the British Society for Extending Fisheries chose Tobermory as the site for a new village and fishing station. Today's town and layout dates largely from that time, though standards of hospitality have greatly risen . . .

Popularly named after the legendary Celtic hero Fingal (*Finn mac cumhal*), who, tradition says, built the island of Staffa, it was locally known as *An Uaimh Bahinn* – 'the musical cave'. Certainly the solitary sound of the sea surge heard within the cave is impressive and has inspired many to improve upon the effect. Accounts tell of bagpipes played, pistols fired and foghorns sounded. In 1886 in perfect weather, the string band from the PS *Chevalier* was towed into the 66-foot-high cave, where it played the Old Hundredth, followed by the national anthem, while tourists stood to attention with their heads uncovered.

The most famous musical visitor to Staffa has been Felix Mendelssohn, who crossed six storm-tossed miles north from Iona to enter its deep basaltic recess on 8 August 1829. In spite of a horrid toothache he was stunned, observing it was 'like the interior of a gigantic organ for the winds and tumultuous waves to play on'. It is said that there and then he jotted down about 20 bars of what has become one of his most popular compositions, *Die Hebriden, op. 26*, known variously and more commonly as the Hebrides or Hebridean Overture, or Fingal's Cave.

The isle of **Colonsay**, which lies west of Jura, is unusually rich in archaeological remains and provable leys. There is the stone circle at Garvard, ruins of the Temple of the Glen in the same place, and the Fort of the Women, where children of the medieval MacPhee chiefs were all said to have been born. Thus mysteries abound, and who knows what secrets are hidden in the very many caves which were inhabited up to 6,000 years ago? There are also standing stones all over the island, medieval churches and standing carved crosses. Virtually attached to Colonsay is **Oronsay**, and there too are ancient remains to be explored.

There are no sheep on Colonsay or Oronsay, but there are certainly plenty of wild goats. These are said to have descended from the survivors of the wreck of the Spanish Armada in 1588. At least 20 of the Spanish Armada were sunk off the west coast of Scotland and Ireland as the fleet attempted to get home to Spain.

The isle of **Jura** was once home to George Orwell, who in the late 1940s, in a house called Barn Hill on the northern end of the island, wrote his great work *1984*. Perhaps he was attracted by living not too far away from one of the world's most terrifying whirlpools, the Corrievreckan, between Jura and the island of Scarba to the north. The pool can at times be heard from the mainland, so loud is the noise of the clashing waters.

Like Islay, Jura was inhabited in quite a considerable way in prehistory and there are several fine sites to be visited. Sites such as Kildalton Cross and Finlaggan must not be missed. Jura is home to well over 5,000 deer, but only 5 per cent of that number in people. It also has many distilleries, including Scotland's most westerly at Bruichladdich, on the shoreline of Loch Indall, where it has been since 1881.

Some have claimed that the site of the Celtic monastery dedicated to St Columba, which is supposed to be on Canna, was in fact more perceptibly identifiable with Jura, and associated with the island named Himba or Hinba. It must be something to do with the angel's breath that escapes the distilleries, but people live a long time on Jura. At a cemetery in Ardlussa in the north of the island there is a stone with this inscription: 'Mary MacCrain, died 1856, aged 128. Descendant of Gillour MacCrain, who kept 180 Christmases in his own house, and who died in the reign of Charles I.'

Islay is quite used to historical visitors being present within its 250 square miles, because a very long time ago the island was used as the headquarters of the Lords of the Isles. The early Lords were of combined Celtic and Norse blood and dominant among them was one Somerled. Their territory passed into the entity of Scotland in 1266, but thereafter there was continual internecine warfare, very often involving the different branches of the MacDonald clan. MacDonald assumed the title 'Lord of the Isles' in the fourteenth century, basing himself on Islay, but the clan chief was not officially acknowledged by the Scottish crown for another century. At the height of their power the Lords of the Isles controlled all the western isles of Scotland and large parts of the western seaboard. The end came for the Lordship and their ownerships in 1493 when forfeit of the land to the crown was completed.

By the time the Lords had arrived, Islay had already seen much prehistoric activity, and as a result the island has many duns, brochs, cairns, standing stones and circles.

Islay is where Prince Charles made an unplanned aircraft landing on 29 June 1994; this just might have been another royal aircraft disaster for historians to file away, but happily this was not so. Later that day he told children at a local school: 'It wasn't quite a crash. We went off the end of the runway, unfortunately. It is not something I recommend happening all the time; unfortunately it did.' No doubt he was helped in his recovery from the incident by his visit to the Laphroaig distillery.

The island of **Arran** is reached by courtesy of the car ferry operators Caledonian MacBrayne, a company which was originally founded by David MacBrayne in 1851. They have a much-appreciated monopoly of travel throughout the Western Isles; indeed, there is a popular rhyme which goes as follows:

> The earth belongs unto the Lord
> And all that it contains,
> Excepting all the Western Isles
> And they are all MacBrayne's.

Arran, divided by the famous string road which goes from Brodick and its castle on the east, across Machry Moor with its Bronze Age standing stones, to Machry on the west coast, is 20 miles from north to south and contains some fascinating and mysterious archaeological remains. These include the Bronze Age ring cairn called Kilpatrick Dun, the Kilmoray Cairns and the Auchagallon Stone Circle, which consists of 15 red sandstone blocks.

Up in the north there's the magic, lonely and beautiful Lochranza Castle, which was made famous by Sir Walter Scott in his *Lord of the Isles*. In the south-west is the so-called King's Cave at Drumadoorn, just north of Blackwaterfoot, which is where Robert the Bruce is famously supposed to have observed a spider at work . . . and was encouraged to 'try' one more time to advance his cause.

Off the coast in the south-east stands **Holy Island**, which is now owned by the monastery of Samye Ling (described in chapter two). Under the leadership of Lama Yeshie, the island has been restored and turned into two major retreat centres, one for men and one for women, where monks will soon be able to spend up to three years, three months and three days seeking self-realisation. Tourists may well be discouraged by the fact that there are to be no dogs, no fires and no alcohol on the island.

Holy Island is so named because a natural cave there was once the retreat of a Culdee anchorite called St Molaise; this small island in the mouth of Lamlash Bay, therefore, is strangely about to relive its history.

Chapter Nine

MONSTERS, GHOULIES AND MURDERS MOST FOUL

Mermaids are fabulous: half woman, half fish. What kind of fish is not so far recorded, but their existence in Scottish waters is a fact that has persisted through many centuries. Here is a story by J.H. Dixon which he wrote in 1886:

> Roderick Mackenzie, the elderly and much respected boat builder at Port Henderson [in Ross and Cromarty], when a young man went one day to a rocky part of the shore there. Whilst gathering bait he suddenly spied a mermaid asleep among the rocks. Rorie went for that mermaid and succeeded in seizing her by the hair. The poor creature in great embarrassment cried out that if Rorie would let go she would grant him whatever boon he might ask. He requested a pledge that no one should ever be drowned from any boat he might build. On his releasing her the mermaid promised that this should be so. The promise has been kept throughout Rorie's long business career — his boats still defy the stormy winds and waves.

Mermaids are of a gentle sort, and it is said that for proof you go and watch them frolicking about in the midday sun beyond the beach at Sandwood Bay, the north-westernmost beach in the country — before they return home to the islets of Am Balg.

For those who know about them, water bulls are less gentle. Around Glencoe you will be advised that they lurk in Lochs Llundavra and Achgriachtan.

Poet and novelist James Hogg (1770–1835) gained his natural affinity with animals when he was a boy, living on a farm in Ettrick Forest, Selkirkshire, and constantly tending sheep. Sir Walter Scott, among many, recognised this simple farmer's son's talent for writing. He became a prominent figure in Edinburgh literary society, and was a co-founder of *Blackwood's Magazine*. He took to styling himself 'the King of the Fairy and Mountain School', and was a constant contributor to John Wilson's Blackwood's series *Noctes Ambrosianae* (1822–35). Wilson's name was in reality Christopher North. The pseudonym Hogg employed for his pieces was 'The Ettrick Shepherd', and it has stuck to him ever since.

James Hogg wrote this, of a water cow which hid for most of its time in the depths of St Mary's Loch, south-west of Selkirk, when he must have stayed at that famous literary drinking outpost on the loch, Tibbie Shiel's Inn. Tibbie was married to a Westmoreland mole-catcher, who probably bored him into written recollections:

> A farmer in Bowerhope once got a breed of herd, which he kept for many years until they multiplied exceedingly. And he never had any cattle drove so well, until once, on some outrage or disrespect on the farmer's part towards them, the old dam came out of the lake one pleasant March evening and gave such a row that all the surrounding hills shook again; upon which her progeny, nineteen in number, followed her all quietly into the loch, and were never more seen.

Stories abound in the Highlands and islands of water horses, or kelpies, as they are often called. (They are known as 'nuggles' in the Shetlands, where the Kelpie Fitful Head, ridden by Black Eric, is still recalled.)

There have been more than 30 sightings of a kelpie in Loch Morar, north-west of Fort William, and this is perhaps so because the water is marvellously clear at this, Britain's deepest freshwater lake (1,017 feet). Most accounts seem to confirm that the kelpie is a dark brown or dark grey colour, and it could be up to 30 feet long. One of the strange aspects of this beast is that the locals are very reluctant to discuss any probable sightings of it.

The earliest known sighting of a 'strange creature' was in 565, when, according to St Adamnan, St Columba drove back 'a great beast' when it was attempting to attack a local villager. The great beast of Loch Awe (*Beathach Mor Loch Obha*) has not been seen for many centuries, but in legend is a far more terrifying creature than that which is supposed to dwell in the depths of Loch Ness. It broke up ice in the winter, and made the most terrifying noise in doing so. It was apparently a kind of cross between an eel with 12 legs and a horse, which is a little difficult to comprehend.

The initials in the stretch of pavement in St Andrews are those of Patrick Hamilton. He was influenced by the teachings of Martin Luther and propagated his doctrines in the university. For this he was tried for heresy, found guilty and burned at the stake on this spot on 29 February 1528, at the age of 24.

☆ ★ ☆ ★ ☆ ★ ☆

On 30 April 1933, the editor of the *Inverness Courier* had before him on his desk an account by a local correspondent of a creature apparently living in Loch Ness. Dr Barron is supposed to have remarked: 'We can't go on calling this thing a creature. If it's as big as people say, then it must be a real monster.' And so it is now called.

Part of the text, by Alex Campbell, printed in the paper the next day, read as follows:

> Now, however, comes the news that the beast has been seen once more, for on Friday of last week a well-known businessman who lives near Inverness, and his wife . . . when motoring along the northern side of the Loch were startled to see a tremendous upheaval on the Loch . . . The creature disported itself for fully a minute, its body resembling that of a whale, and the water cascading and churning like a simmer cauldron . . . Both onlookers confessed that there was something uncanny about the whole thing, for they realised that this was no ordinary denizen of the deep.

Sir Compton Mackenzie (1883–1972; author of *Whisky Galore*) claimed that he had seen the so-called monster a few days before this account was published, and thought it was a grey seal. The witnesses referred to were local hoteliers at Drumnadrochit overlooking Urquhart Bay in the loch, and were worried lest they were seen to be courting publicity. They developed the theory that the new road along the northern shore of Loch Ness, which had been begun a year before, perhaps disturbed the monster in his deeps, because rock-blasting was inevitably necessary to make a straight road.

I have no firm views about whether such a monster exists, but readers are recommended to repair to three good viewing points to test the subject for themselves. These are at Foyers, Fort Augustus and below the ruined and romantic Castle Urquhart.

The Scotsman, on 6 July 1934, printed a further account of a sighting which should perhaps be watched out for even today:

> I was working on the Glendoe Estate [at the southern end of Loch Ness] about 9 am, and from a small hill overlooking the loch I saw the calm surface suddenly

This shallow waterfall and pool is on the River Snizort in the grounds of the Skeabost House Hotel on Skye. The waterfall is known as the Cauldron of the Heads. In a battle in 1528 the defeated MacLeods made a last desperate stand right here against the MacDonalds. The bodies of the slain were floated in this pool.

broken by a most amazing beast. It was at least 30 feet long and as its length continued to emerge, I could distinctly see a number of humps. I was looking almost straight down on it and when it first appeared I counted twelve humps, each a foot out of the water. It moved off towards Glendoe Pier, and on one occasion lifted its head and neck out of the water and shook itself. I then saw something extending for about four feet from the head down the neck, dark-coloured, rather like a mane. The day was so clear that I could distinctly see drops of water as they fell when the monster shook itself. It reached Glendoe Pier and stretched its neck out of the water, where a stream enters the loch. It did not actually come ashore but seemed to be hunting about the edge and I cannot see how it could move as it did without using flippers or feet.

Loch Ness contains more water than all the reservoirs and lakes of England and Wales put together (265,000,000,000 cubic feet), being 24 miles long, averaging one mile wide and up to 820 feet deep. It receives seven rivers: the Farigaig, Foyers, Tarff, Oich, Moriston, Coilte and Enrick. One of the few other certain facts which has emerged recently is that the famous picture of the monster taken in 1934 by Colonel Frank Wilson, a British Army surgeon, was a fake. He refused to allow anything to be published about his activities until after his death in 1994, and it may well be that the so-called Loch Ness Monster is the least mysterious object to be found in the pages of this book.

Hector Boece recorded in his history of Scotland, which was published in 1527, that he had been told by a certain Sir Duncan Campbell that:

out of Garloch, a loch of Argyle, came a terrible beast as big as a greyhound, puted like a gander and struck down great trees with the length of his tail; and slew three men quickly who were hunting with three strokes of his tail; and were it not for the remnant of the hunters climbed up in the strong oaks, they had all been slain in some way. After the slaughter of these men it fled speedily to the loch. Sundry prudent men

How to find the monster in Loch Ness.

The skull of Robert the Bruce in Dunfermline Abbey.

believed great trouble would follow in Scotland because of the appearance of this beast, for such had been seen before, and great trouble always followed soon after.

A history called *The Chronicles of Fortingael* described how in 1570 'there was ane monstrous fish, seen in Lochfyne, having a great een in the head thereof and at times would stand above the water as high as the mast of a ship; and the said had upon the head thereof two croons . . . whilk was reportit by wise men, that the same was one sighn and toekn of ane sudden alteration in this realm.'

There are rumours even today that there is a great beast in the depths of Loch Awe and another in Loch Rannoch. During their visit to the island of Raasay in 1773, Boswell recorded one story which their guide of the day told to Dr Johnson and himself:

There was a wild beast in it, a sea horse which came and devoured a man's daughter; upon which the man lighted a great fire and had a sow roasted on it, the smell of which attracted the monster. In the fire was put a spit. A man lay concealed behind a low wall of loose stones which extended from the fire over the summit of the hill till it reached the side of the loch. The monster came, and the man with a red-hot spit destroyed it. Malcolm (the guide) showed me the little

hiding place and the row of stones. He did not laugh when he told me this story.

Sir Walter Scott recorded in his *Journal* for 23 November 1827:

Clanronald told us, an instance of Highland credulity, that a set of his kinsmen — Borrodale and others — believing that the fabulous 'water-cow' inhabited a small lake near his house, resolved to drag the monster into day. With this in view they bivouacked by the side of the lake in which they placed, by way of night bait — two small anchors such as belong to boats, each baited with the carcase of a dog, slain for the purpose. They expected the water cow would gorge on this bait and were prepared to drag her ashore the next morning when, to their confusion of face, the baits were found untouched. It is something too late in the day for setting baits for water cows.

Under the heading 'The Sea Serpent in the Highlands', *The Times* printed this story on 6 March 1856:

The village of Leurbost, Parish of Lochs, Lewis [eight miles south-west of Stornoway], is at present the scene of an unusual occurrence. This is no less than the appearance in one of the inland fresh-water lakes of an animal which from its great size and dimensions has not a little puzzled our island naturalists. Some suppose him to be a description of the hitherto mythological water-kelpie; while others refer it to the minute descriptions of the 'sea-serpent', which are revived from time to time in the newspaper columns. It has been repeatedly seen within the last fortnight by crowds of people, many of whom have come from the remotest parts of the parish to witness the uncommon spectacle. The animal is described by some as being in appearance and size like 'a large peat stack', while others affirm that a 'six-oared boat' could pass between the huge fins, which are occasionally visible. All, however, agree in describing its form as that of an eel; and we have heard one, whose evidence we can rely upon, state that in length he supposed it to be about 40 feet. It is probable that it is no more than a conger eel after all, animals of this description having been caught in Highland lakes which have attained huge size. He is currently reported to have swallowed a blanket inadvertently left on the bank by a girl herding cattle. A sportsman ensconced himself with a rifle in the vicinity of the loch during a whole day, hoping to get a shot, but did no execution.

☆ ★ ☆ ★ ☆ ★ ☆

Frae Witches, Warlocks, an' Wurricoes,
An' Evil Spirits, an' a' Things
That gan Bump i' the Nicht,
Guid Lord, deliver us!

Traditional

Late one afternoon in December 1995, in the bar area of the County Hotel in Ayr's elegant Wellington Square, a temporary barman was preparing for the evening's custom – when he suddenly caught sight of someone of whom he had heard much. It was the Grey Nun. The ghostly presence hovered near him for a few seconds as the room cooled, and then vanished.

The Grey Nun had been seen a number of times on the top floor of the hotel, which is composed of four houses and dates back to the Square's construction in 1815. There are 'crawl spaces' between the old houses, and it is in them that the Grey Nun is said to reside. The proprietors have told me that there have been odd occurrences inside securely locked rooms up there; a cup and saucer have been found on the floor precisely in the middle of the room – ready perhaps for a purvey, a Scottish funeral breakfast.

Auld Ayr, wham ne'er a town surpasses
For honest men and bonny lasses.

Robert Burns, 'The Ayrshire Poet'

This where a young woman of Ayr's prominent Osborne family was burnt to death for witchcraft in the mid-seventeenth century by the ancient (and long-destroyed) Malt Cross. Perhaps the Grey Nun tends her soul.

Braemar was once called St Andrews. In the early sixteenth century the Earl of Mar acquired land in the area, and so we have Braemar, a village, now a town, where Robert Louis Stevenson wrote most of *Treasure Island* in a modest house overlooking an ancient preaching cross. The churchyard of St Andrews in Braemar contains the family vault of the Farquharsons of Invercauld, the mansion in the parish whence went the Earl of Mar's call, the 'fiery cross', to all Highlanders in 1715.

In that churchyard one John Farquharson, known as 'The Black Colonel', and perhaps the person who shot the self-styled 'Baron of Brackley' in 1666, was laid to rest. But that is not what he wanted at all.

Farquharson had expressed a desire to be buried in an ancient graveyard beside the ruins of Inverey Castle, the old Farquharson *fortalice* which was razed to the ground by royalist troops after the Battle of Killiecrankie in July 1689. On the day after its interment in the large family vault, the coffin mysteriously appeared above the ground beside the vault. It was quickly placed back inside, but on the next day it reappeared again. Again it was put back. For the third time the Black Colonel's coffin reappeared. John Farquharson had resurrected himself three times. He had made his point, and now he lies where he desired.

It is strange to relate that there are many ghosts in Scotland known as 'The Green Lady'. One is reputed to be that of Lady Jean Drummond, who drowned in marshes near Ardblair Castle in Blairgowrie; she is seen both there and at Newton Castle, another nearby

The lovely, lonely Castle Stalker, near Appin, the scene of the famous murder.

Cumberland's Stone at Culloden. The Duke of Cumberland stood on it while commanding the Hanoverian troops during the bloody Battle of Culloden (1746), which lasted just 68 minutes. More Scotsmen fought for him than for the Jacobite cause.

family home. Another Green Lady dwells in Fyvie Castle; she has her own room there, quite reasonably called 'The Haunted Chamber'. A complete skeleton of an unknown person was once discovered in it . . .

Easily the oldest location of a Green Lady ghost is in Argyll, north of Oban, in Dunstaffnage Castle, allegedly founded by a Pictish king or an early chief of a branch of the Dalriada. And quite the grandest building in which to encounter a Green Lady is Stirling Castle. She is said to have been one of Mary, Queen of Scots' maids, and to have saved the Queen's life after the draperies around her bed caught fire the night after the christening of her son, later James VI, in December 1566. The Queen had forced the Privy Council to contribute £12,000 towards the cost of the christening because, reads a document of the time, 'sum of the grettest princes in Christendome hes ernestlie requirit of our soveranis that be thair ambassatouris thai may be witnessis and gosseppis at the baptisme of thair Majesteis derrist sone'.

On the eve of the Battle of Flodden, James IV (1473–1513) was pleased to be present at a service in St Michael's Church as the sun set in Linlithgow. An apparition appeared before him in the form of a pale and ghostly old man in a long gown and holding a staff, who warned him please, please not to march south, or he would be defeated and killed in a terrible battle with the English at Flodden Field.

It is said that the ghost was also witnessed by Sir David Lyndsay (*c.*1486–1555), statesman and royal confidant. The king chose to ignore him, and he led the planned march. The prophecy came to pass. He died on the field of battle on 9 September 1513, as the English, under the Earl of Surrey, achieved their victory.

Scottish history is gory, and has been trailed in blood by its heroes and victims. Massacre and murder were routine territorial trading practices in the old days, and it is easy to understand the centuries-old belief in Scotland that if a man is murdered, his soul, in ghostly form, lingers on earth until his pre-ordained natural span expires. Thus are the guilty the more easily haunted.

In this connection, the 'royals' in Scotland have had a hard time, going right back to 954 when Malcolm I was killed in battle. Malcolm III (*c.*1031–*c.*1093) met an untimely end at Alnwick, and Macbeth was killed on 15 August 1057 by the forces of Malcolm III. Alexander III fell over a cliff on his horse on a dark night in 1286 at what is now called Kinghorn, on the north shore of the Firth of Forth.

Sir William Wallace was not a royal but certainly suffered under one, after he led the resistance to English invaders under Edward I in 1297. He was captured, tried in London at Westminster Hall (which still stands), condemned to death, hanged on 22 August 1305, drawn, beheaded and then quartered. Those quarters were despatched to Newcastle, Berwick, Stirling and Perth.

James I was assassinated on 20 February 1437 in a monastery in Perth. It happened because he couldn't use an escape tunnel on account of the fact that it had been bricked up a few days earlier to prevent tennis balls, of all things, falling into it.

James II – called James of the Fiery Face because of a disfiguring birthmark – was present when young at the infamous Black Dinner at Edinburgh Castle when the sixth Earl of Douglas was murdered. He personally murdered the eighth Earl in 1452, and received his own violent end in a siege at Roxburgh on 3 August 1460. He was standing next to a massive cannon, known as 'The Lion', when it burst and the fragments killed him. A yew tree was planted by the sixth Duke of Roxburghe to mark the spot.

The next royal assassination was that of James III. He fled from the Battle of Sauchieburn (less than two miles from Bannockburn), showing no bravery against insurgent nobles and their 18,000-strong army. He fell from his horse, was badly injured and, fearing the worst, called for a priest. A man claiming to be one was soon found and brought to the king. James III was then stabbed in the heart many times.

Mary, Queen of Scots (daughter of James V and Mary of Guise, and born in 1542) plotted endlessly against her cousin Elizabeth of England whom she wanted to replace. Some say this scheming woman connived in the murder of her husband, Lord Darnley (1546–1567), at Kirk o' Field with the help of the fourth Earl of Bothwell, whom she married three months later. However, she failed to have the incriminating 'casket letters' disposed of.

After yet another death plot, Mary was condemned to death by the Star Chamber in Westminster on 25 October 1586. Three hundred people watched her being executed on 8 February 1587. The man with the axe held her head aloft – and from it fell an auburn wig. The hair beneath was cropped and grey. And then a Skye terrier ran out from under her skirts, and could not be comforted.

The Appin Murder, one of Scotland's most famous, had its origins in the '45 and Culloden. On 17 March 1752, a bill was passed in law providing for forfeited Jacobite estates to become the property of the English Crown, and their revenues to be used for the improvement of the Highlands. The latter notion was worthy but never occurred.

The Stewarts of Appin, in Argyll, and the Camerons of Lochaber had both supported Prince Charles Edward Stuart ('Bonnie Prince Charlie') – but the Stewarts loathed the Campbells. Colin Campbell of Glenure (whose mother was a Cameron) was not at Culloden, but gained the appointment of Government Factor for the lands of the Stewarts of Ardsheal in Appin, and also of the Camerons of Locheil at Lochaber. He had as an assistant James Stewart, half-brother of the exiled laird of Ardsheal.

The ex-Jacobite James Stewart was soon forced to move to Acharn, south-west of Kenmore in Perthshire, from Auchindarroch, north-west of Lochgilphead in Argyll, due to Colin Campbell's mismanagement of the estates and his suspected sympathy for the Jacobite cause.

Those who have read Robert Louis Stevenson's evocative and thrilling novels *Kidnapped* and *Catriona* will recall 'the Red Fox'; Colin Campbell was known as Red Colin; David Balfour's friend is Alan Breck. A real Allan 'Breck' Stewart (*breac* means 'speckled' or 'pockmarked') was born in Appin, joined the army, was taken prisoner at Prestonpans, changed sides and joined the Jacobites, and fled to France. The Camerons were his maternal cousins, and he was a foster son of James Stewart ('James of the Glens'), Colin Campbell's assistant.

The day of the Appin Murder was 14 May 1752. Colin Campbell had left Maryburgh (now called Fort William) heading for Appin to oversee forced evictions of Jacobite tenants from estates he managed. At about five o'clock that afternoon, as he neared Lettermore and its slate quarries, north-west of Ballachulish, he was shot dead. His servant spotted a man scuttling away. The crime was reported to James Stewart, who declined (crucially) to visit the site of the murder, and exclaimed that if he did so he would be found guilty, even though he was not.

Suspicion swung between 'James of the Glens' and his foster son Allan 'Breck' Stewart. At first the latter was blamed, because he was known to have been fishing in the area at the time and subsequently vanished. A description of him was issued:

About 5 feet 10 inches high; his face much marked with the small Pox, black bushy hair put up in a bag, a little in-knee'd, round shouldered, has full black eyes, and is about 30 years of age.

Not a pleasant description. Allan 'Breck' Stewart was never seen again, and it is said that he died much later in France.

James Stewart was arrested and his trial commenced on 21 September 1752, in a courtroom that offered him no hope of reprieve whatsoever. For it took place in Inveraray, home of the Campbells; 11 of the 15 jurymen were of that clan, and the presiding judge, the Duke of Argyll, was plainly out for Stewart's blood as an accessory to the murder.

'James of the Glens' protested his innocence throughout, but on 8 November he was led to a gibbet beside the Ballachulish ferry. There he made a speech steeped in humility, which ended: 'Come, Lord Jesus, come quickly.' As he walked to the scaffold, he recited out loud the 35th Psalm, which begins: 'Plead thou my cause, O Lord, with them that strive with me: and fight thou against them that fight against me.' A reading of the psalm ensures a feeling that he was certainly innocent.

His body was left rotting on that gibbet until it blew down in January 1755. Within a month his skeleton was up again, all wired together. He is now buried in an unmarked grave in an old chapel near Duror, five miles south of the gibbet.

It so happened that the Julian calendar replaced the Gregorian one in Scotland on 3 September 1752, and so the luckless James Stewart in fact lived 11 days fewer than his dates indicate.

The name of the true guilty party is said to be passed down from generation to generation of Stewarts. I wonder whether the name MacColl is kept hidden away at the back of a drawer, somewhere south of Ballachulish and north of Loch Etive?

☆ ★ ☆ ★ ☆ ★ ☆

There are separate memorial stones for the clans Stewart of Appin and Cameron of Locheil on grassy mounds on the battlefield of Culloden (correctly Drummossie Muir), marking the bloody event of 16 April 1746. Very full accounts of this day have been published, and the facts are horrid. The royalists lost only about 50 men, while the Jacobites must have had over 1,200 men killed – although most of those numbers were massacred *after* the battle. The conflict itself only lasted 68 minutes, so hopeless had Bonnie Prince Charlie's cause become.

That last pitched battle on British soil, in which more Scots fought against than for the Stuart cause, had been the subject of a premonition by the Braham Seer when he visited Culloden 100 years before: 'This black moor, 'ere many generations have passed, shall be stained with the best blood of Scotland.'

A union of a kind between England and Scotland was clearly on the way, as Bonnie Prince Charlie (1720–88) finally fled from Scotland on 20 September 1746. He was to lead a dissolute life, and ended his unhappy days in Rome.

Another seer, this time earlier, foresaw the real beginning of the political manoeuvres which resulted in the Act of Union of 1 May 1707. Thomas Rymour of Erceldoune (*c.*1220–*c.*1297), known as Thomas the Rymer, became widely known after his prophecies were published in 1603. He was interested in King Arthur, and this took him to Drumelzier, south-west of Peebles, and to a field, near the village churchyard, in which Merlin the Wizard was apparently buried. Thomas recorded a perception there:

When Tweed and Powsail meet at Merlin's grave,
Scotland and England shall one monarch have.

On 24 March 1603, following weeks of heavy rain, the River Tweed dramatically overflowed its banks and its waters, for the first time, merged with those of Powsail Burn, above which Drumelzier stood. On that very same day, Queen Elizabeth I of England died, and thus James VI of Scotland became also James I of England.

☆ ★ ☆ ★ ☆ ★ ☆

Here is what Halliday Sutherland, author of *Arches of the Years*, had to say about an acquaintance who understood witches, superstition, and their involvement of death:

He had also known a witch, and had killed her. She had lived three miles up the glen in a small croft, now in ruins, and at night had gone about in the form of a hare. One moonlight night he had seen this hare running away from the door of the byre, and in the morning one of the cows stopped giving milk.

The next night he loaded his gun and over the charge rammed down a sixpence, because a silver bullet is the only bullet that will kill a witch. Then he waited behind a wall overlooking the byre, and in the moonlight saw the hare coming back. He fired. She gave a scream and fled on three legs, trailing a broken right hind-leg behind her. On the following day no smoke was rising from the house of the witch, and when neighbours entered they found her groaning on her bed. When the doctor came he said her right thigh was broken below the hip-joint. The witch explained that she had fallen in her room. Mr. Cameron knew better, and in a few days she was dead. If the doctor had cut into her he would have found a sixpence in her thigh!

The old church dedicated to St Andrew by the harbour at North Berwick was the scene of a terrible trial of 94 witches and six wizards in the year 1591. Before it they danced in the kirkyard to the sound of Geilie Duncan's playing on a Jew's harp, and then (according to a contemporary account):

the devil startit up himself in the pulpit, like ane meikle black man, and callit every man by name, and every ane answerit, 'Here, Master'. On his command they openit up the graves, twa within, and one without the Kirk, and took off the joints of their fingers, taes, and knees, and partit them amang them; and Agnes Simpson gat for her part ane winding-sheet and twa joints, whilk she tint negligently.

Between 1479 and 1722, more than 4,000 people — most of them women, though not all — were burnt at the stake in Scotland for being witches. They were very often strangled first; Scots for strangulation is *worryit*.

In extreme cases of torture in the eighteenth century an Iron Maiden was sometimes employed. This was a ten-foot-high steel hinged body case, with sharp nails sticking into the *interior*, threatening all parts of the body. To be forced naked inside it and to see and hear the great steel pronged door slowly being closed must have produced more deaths by heart attack than by the nails. The very last intended victim was an ancestor of mine, Robert Balfour. He got clean away in 1710.

One of the nastiest Scotsmen who ever lived did so in Galloway, and commenced his heinous activities from a coastal cave near Ballantrae at the start of the fifteenth century. He has come down through the history of crime with the name Sawney Bean. He took up with a female of equivalent character and they quickly produced eight sons and six daughters; these in turn entirely incestuously bred 18 grandsons and 14 granddaughters. They all existed from the spoils of robbery, murdered indiscriminately and were cannibals. Their cave was so remote, dark and awful that it was very many years before Sawney Bean and his familial crew were captured, executed and dismembered (the men first, and slowly) at the Mercat Cross in Leith, Edinburgh.

The last public execution in Britain was in Glasgow on 28 July 1865. The convicted murderer was Edward Pritchard, a tall, balding man with a long beard but no moustache to go with it, who professed to be a doctor but probably wasn't, was universally loathed, and poisoned his wife, mother-in-law and at least one mistress. He couldn't get on with women, apparently. Over 80,000 people saw him hang from the gallows at the bottom of the Saltmarket, facing Nelson's Monument in the Green.

The last witch to be judicially burned in Scotland was Janet Horne. She perished by the golf links in Littletown, Dornoch, in 1722, found guilty of transforming her daughter into a pony and then having it shod by the devil. The Witch Stone commemorates this sad tale.

The beautiful Cathedral at Dornoch is known as such in spite of the fact that it has no bishop because it is a Presbyterian Church of Scotland. Much of the building was burned down in 1570 during a feud between the Murrays of Dornoch and the MacKays of Strathnaver, but the tower and some Gothic arches survived the disaster. Then came 5 November 1605: the day of the Gunpowder Plot down in London. Sir Robert Gordon (historian; 1580–1656) linked that event to a terrible storm which brought down the tower and more:

The same verie night that this execrable plott should have been put in execution all the inner stone pillars of the north syd of the body of the cathedral church at Dornogh — lacking the rooff before — were blowen from the verie roots and foundation quyt and clein over the outer walls of the church: such as hath seine the same. These great winds did even then prognosticate and forshew some great treason to be at hand; and as the devill was busie then to trouble the ayre, so was he busie by these his fyrebrands to trouble the estate of Great Britane.

Dornoch Cathedral is full of Sutherlands (whose history Gordon wrote) — 16 earls in the south transept, and more in a mausoleum beneath the choir. This

127

provides the answer to the puzzle of why the *piscina* in the south wall, a remnant of pre-Reformation days, is not at waist height (for the convenient disposal of excess consecrated wine after Mass) but at floor level. The Sutherlands, in their bulk, had the floor levels raised.

Into the chancel walls are set some finely carved stone Mortality Stones from the eighteenth century. On them are carved skulls, coffins, hour glasses, sexton's spades and bells for ringing at funerals. All are reminders that we should number our days, as we are merely passing through.

THE BUSH ABOON TRAQUAIR

This poem was published in 1864, and is by John Campbell Shairp (1819–1885), who was educated at Glasgow University and Balliol College, Oxford, where he won the Newdigate Prize and eventually became Professor of Poetry. He was later a professor of Latin and Greek at Glasgow and St Andrews, and Edinburgh University conferred upon him a doctorate of literature in the year before he died.

Will ye gang wi' me and fare
To the bush aboon Traquair?
Owre the high Minchmuir we'll up and awa',
This bonny summer noon.
While the sun shines fair aboon,
And the licht sklents saftly doun on holm and ha'.

And what would ye do there,
At the bush aboon Traquair?
A lang drierch road, ye had better let it be;
Save some auld skrunts o' birk
I' the hillside lirk,
There's nocht i' the warld for man to see.

But the blithe lilt o' that air,
'The Bush aboon Traquair,'
I need nae mair, it's eneuch for me;
Owre my cradle its sweet chime
Cam' sughin' frae auld time,
Sae tide what may, I'll awa' and see.

And what saw ye there
At the bush aboon Traquair?
Or what did ye hear that was worth your heed?
I heard the cushies croon
Through the gowden afternoon,
And the Quair burn singing doun to the Vale o'
Tweed,

And birks saw I three or four,
Wi' grey moss bearded owre,
The last that are left o' the birken shaw,
Whar mony a simmer e'en
Fond lovers did convene,
Thae bonny, bonny gloamin's that are lang awa'.

Frae mony a but and ben,
By muirland, holm, and glen,
They cam' ane hour to spen' on the greenwood
    sward;
But lang hae lad an' lass
Been lying 'neath the grass,
The green, green grass o' Traquair kirkyard.

They were blest beyond compare,
When they held their trysting there
Amang thae greenest hills shone on by the sun.
And when they wan a rest,
The lownest and the best,
I' Traquair kirkyard when a' was dune.

Now the birks to dust may rot,
Names o' luvers be forgot,
Nae lads and lasses there ony mair convene;
But the blithe lilt o' yon air
Keeps the bush aboon Traquair,
And the luve that ance was there, aye fresh and green.

Chapter Ten

STORIES FROM PALACES, CASTLES AND OTHER GREAT HOMES

It is said that there are over 1,000 castles in Scotland, and that each of them is inhabited by at least one ghost. It is fortunate that the pale troop cannot make plain their feelings in words, because the histories of these domestic strongholds are mostly brutish. All manner of crimes have been perpetrated in the causes of clans, and the behavioural characteristics of several of them – the Black Douglases, for example – scarcely alter down the generations.

Even great brooding ruins have their stories to tell, and strange powers lurk within their walls. Arbroath Abbey will be mentioned below. Slains Castle in Cruden Bay, Aberdeenshire, now roofless, was, to quote Dr Johnson who visited the Erroll seat in 1773, 'built upon the margin of the sea so that the walls of one of the towers seem only a continuation of a perpendicular rock, the foot of which is beaten by the waves'. In 1895, Bram Stoker started writing *Dracula* in Cruden Bay, using Slains Castle as his inspiration for the vampire's castle. Try a walk from the car park up to the castle ruins on a wild and stormy night, and you might come up with a story of your own.

Castle Sween, which crowns a rocky promontory on the eastern side of Loch Sween in Knapsdale, Argyll, is regarded as the oldest stone castle on the Scottish mainland. It was probably constructed early in the eleventh century by Sweno, Prince of Denmark. The Treaty of Tarbert of 1098 confirmed that the Hebrides and Kintyre belonged to the Norse kingdom, an unsatisfactory arrangement which was ended by the Battle of Largs on 2 October 1263.

Another ruin is Dunnottar Castle, Stonehaven, Kincardineshire, on a site fortified as far back as the seventh century. More than 100 covenanters were incarcerated there in 1695 during Argyll's rebellion.

Curses abound within Scotland's dressed and assembled stones. One of them reigns in the Penkill Room, Penkill Castle, near Girvan, Ayrshire. In 1697, Sir William Anstruther built the renaissance-style Elie House not far from the harbour at Elie, East Neuk, Fife, and near the town of Anstruther. It stayed in family hands until the 1850s. There is a local legend that a gypsy placed a curse on the family because it had destroyed the village of Balclevie, saying that only six generations of Anstruthers would dwell in Elie House. And that is exactly what happened.

Some great residences in Scotland have different appeals. Delgatie Castle, north-east of Turriff, boasts some painted ceilings which, unsung, are among the finest in the whole world. It has just been opened to the public for the first time, after a brief period of nearly 950 years.

Some houses in Scotland are not 'great', but important to some. A gardener and his family once lived in a humble cottage in Kirkbean in Kirkcudbrightshire. They were always familiar with the sea, as the village overlooks the Solway Firth. One son in the family was John Paul Jones (born John Paul; 1747–1792), and he was to be the founder of the mighty US Navy. That cottage is destined to be a museum.

Charles Rennie Mackintosh (1868–1928) is one of Scotland's greatest and most influential architects and designers, and an outstanding exponent of the Art Nouveau style. It is, again, not a great home, but his Hill House, in Helensburgh, north-west of Glasgow, is a startling achievement. 'Toshie' designed the whole edifice, and contents, in 1903–1904 for the publisher Walter Blackie.

The following selection of thrilling dwellings, offered in alphabetical order, is purely eclectic – as it has to be with 1,000 and more of them from which to choose. I have not stayed with Cicero's advice in his *De Officiis* – *Ex malis eligere minima oportere*: 'Of evil one should select the least.'

Sir Walter Scott (1771–1832) and all his literary works have done more, whether to general approval or not, to 'promote Scotland' than any other single writer. It is therefore singularly appropriate that I commence this gory ramble with **Abbotsford**, his mansion two miles west of Melrose, beside the River Tweed, the sight of which was his last.

No less than six of his brothers and sisters (out of 12) died in infancy. Walter caught polio when a baby, became lame and was packed off to a family farm near Kelso to become strong. Thus it was that traditional

Borders' legends, songs, stories and doubtful rumours arrived in his fertile imagination, and were the making of him. In 1812 he bought a lowly four-bedroomed cottage called Cartley Hole (*not* Hall, as some literature has it), and after its eventual demolition and his gradual acquisition of lands around it, Abbotsford was created. Scott created the name from the abbots of nearby Melrose Abbey (home to the heart but not the body of Robert the Bruce) and a shallow local crossing in the Tweed which they used for the passage of their cattle, and drew inspiration from the fact that Cartley Hole was a reputed haunt of 'Thomas the Rymer'.

With an industry he applied equally to his enormous literary output, Walter Scott (who was made a baronet in 1820) set about creating his dream home for himself and his French wife Charlotte Charpentier (whom he married, with typical imaginative verve, on Christmas Eve, 1797). Between 1817 and 1821 a Scottish 'baronial pile' arose. He implanted copies of what he admired but could never possess: a mantelpiece from Melrose Abbey, carved oak work from the Palace of Holyrood, a gateway from Linlithgow Palace, roofwork from Rosslyn Chapel, oak panelling from Dunfermline Palace, furniture given to him by the Pope, George III and IV, and Lord Byron. The baronetcy was not for the lack of fame. Early shades of William Randolph Hearst and San Simeon.

Sir Walter Scott became too closely involved with both his publishers and their printers, and in 1826 he faced financial ruin only months after his wife suddenly died. He spent the rest of his life, in an honourable attempt to avoid bankruptcy, trying to pay off his debts, became ill, and died in his dining room on an elevated bed (to obtain the view of the Tweed and beyond) on 21 September 1832. Inexplicable disturbances in the night have been occasionally heard ever since. Scott had ignored the old belief that it is unlucky to change the name of a house.

Arbroath was the model for Fairport in Sir Walter Scott's novel *The Antiquary* (1816). As abbots once lived there, I consider that **Arbroath Abbey** qualifies for its place in this chapter. The Abbot's House was near the south wall of the now-ruined nave in this still remarkably moving place. The abbey was founded by King William the Lion (or Lyon) in 1178, completed in 1233, and dedicated to both St Mary and his friend and martyr Thomas à Becket. Its first monks were from a reformed Benedictine Tyronensian order (originally from Chartres) in Kelso.

The abbey was already in ruins when the tomb of William the Lion was discovered in 1816 during restorations before the high altar. He had been laid to rest there on 9 December 1214.

One of the great events in Scottish history has been the Declaration of Independence. It was in the form of a letter, dated 6 April 1320, roundly rebuking Pope John XXII for siding with Edward II of England against Robert I the Bruce, after Edward's defeat by the Scots at the Battle of Bannockburn on 23–24 June 1314. It opened '*Sanctissimo Patri in Christo ac domino, domino Johanni divina providencia Sacrosauncte Romane et Universalis Ecclesie Summo Pontifici, Filii Sui Humiles et devcti*' and there followed the names of its brave and inspired signatories (eight earls and 31 barons).

The original letter has been lost, or is perhaps locked away in the Vatican. The contemporary parchment copy in the Scottish Record Office in Edinburgh embodies some of the finest Latin prose ever to come out of Scotland, with great phrases proclaiming a mighty preference for Scotland's independence. The letter employed surprisingly direct language, and survives as one of the world's greatest affirmations – a rare and lovely word – of a nation's intent. No surprise, then, that it is constantly requoted today.

In August 1951 a splendid pageant was held in the ruins of Arbroath Abbey, in which the signing of the Declaration of Independence was re-enacted. It was inspired by a daring idea. The Stone of Destiny has been mentioned thus in an old rhyme:

Ni fallat fatum, Scoti, quocunque locatum,
Invenient lapidem, regnare tenentur ibidem.

This talisman of Scottish royalty is supposed to have been brought to the Palace of Scone by Kenneth mac Alpin, after he united the Picts and the Scots, from either Dunadd or Dunstaffnage. Incidentally, it is a strange fact that the Stone originally came from Cashel in Ireland, while the Irish stone of Tara was apparently gathered and shaped in Scotland.

In 1296 Edward I summarily removed the Stone of Destiny to London, where the Coronation Chair was constructed to accommodate it. That pageant was inspired by a daring idea which succeeded – with the help of an old Austin Seven. The Stone of Destiny was removed from beneath the Coronation Chair in Westminster Abbey by a group of young Scots on Christmas Day in 1950, driven north in the car, and secreted in a cellar while its future was discussed in high places. After three months a certain decision was made.

On 11 April 1951, Ian Hamilton, Bill Craig and Billy Gray strapped the Stone on to a wooden stretcher,

Traquair House.

Melrose Abbey.

carried it down the nave of Arbroath Abbey and laid it in front of the altar, at the very spot where William the Lion is buried. Scotland Yard detectives were quickly on to the case, retrieved The Stone of Destiny and drove it back to Westminster in a Black Maria. They at least believed it was the Stone.

Ballindalloch Castle, north-east of Grantown, by the Spey, is one of the most beautiful privately owned castles in all Scotland. '1546' is carved on a stone lintel in a bedroom and is taken as the date of the tower where the room is, and the start of the castle's gradual construction. A legend in the Macpherson-Grant family says that foundations (still visible, and this is the strange part) for the castle were originally laid on a nearby hill, but real building never commenced because of an endlessly repeated ghostly message saying 'Build it in the coo-haugh'. And so there it stands today, in the company of the oldest Aberdeen-Angus herd in the world and a doocot dated 1696 with 844 nesting boxes.

Most castles in Scotland have doocots commensurate with their ages. Doos fed on neighbouring farms, and their fresh meat was always appreciated during the long winters. Doo dung cures baldness, but I think one would need a wee dram or

two to stand the thought of such an application. The cure for a fever is much nicer: warm doo hearts should be applied to the feet. Yes. On top of feet where the blue veins run.

One illustrious ancestor of the family is General (James) Grant (1706–1778), who fought at Culloden and then in the American Wars of Independence over the water. In his later years he was a noted *bon viveur*, and always travelled with his cooks. In 1770 he added the north wing to the castle especially to house his favourite French chef. The Macpherson motto is famous: 'Touch not the cat bot a glove'; in other words, wear gloves if you are about to tangle with any member of the clan. This motto is shared with the Mackintosh clan.

Castle Stalker stands alone, forbidding and also forbidden (it is a private residence), on a rocky islet in Loch Linnhe, off the south-western Appin peninsula. It was built by Duncan Stewart of Appin (see 'The Appin Murder' in chapter nine) at the end of the fifteenth century, and it possesses a cold and hideous prison vault. James IV's arms are carved over the entrance, facing a bridge which was once a drawbridge, because he used the place as a hunting

Arbroath Abbey.

Glamis Castle.

lodge. It derives its present name from *Stalchair*, the Castle of The Hunter.

In the graveyard at Portnacroish, the nearest mainland village, there is an inscription on a stone which reads:

> 1468. Above this spot was fought the bloody battle of Stalc, in which many hundreds fell, when the Stewarts and the MacLarens, their allies, in defence of Dugald, Chief of Appin, son of Sir John Stewart, Lord of Lorne and Innermeath, defeated the combined forces of the MacDougalls and the MacFarlanes.

The battle took place in the nearby Hollow of Treachery. Difficult times.

A total of 63 thanedoms once existed in Scotland. Saxons adapted the Norse word *thegn*, which meant a trusted servant of the king. The most notable thane today is probably the young Thane of Cawdor, whose lair above a rocky burn is **Cawdor Castle**, between Nairn and Culloden's bloody battlefield. The Charter of Thanage was first received from Robert the Bruce in 1310 by one William Calder.

The Calders of Calder are said to be descended from a brother of Macbeth (king in 1040–1057). The building of the Tower of Calder (the heart of today's Cawdor Castle) started in 1454. The ninth thane was actually a thaness called Muriel. This is an old account of what happened to her in 1499:

> She, still a child, was walking with her nurse near the Tower of Calder, when she was captured by a party of 60 Campbells. Her uncles pursued and overtook the division to whose care she had been entrusted, and would have rescued her but for the presence of mind of Campbell of Innerliever, who, seeing their approach, inverted a large camp-kettle as if to conceal her, and, bidding his seven sons defend it to the death, hurried on with his prize. The young men were all slain, and when the Calders lifted up the kettle, no Muriel was there.
>
> Meanwhile so much time had been gained, that further pursuit was useless. The nurse, at the moment the child was seized, bit off a joint of her little finger in order to mark her identity and scored her hip with a key — no needless precaution, as appears from Campbell of Auchinbreck's answer to the question, 'What was to be done should the child die before she came of marriageable age?'

The legendary Bear Gates on the original driveway to Traquair House. They are never opened.

'She can never die', said he, 'as long as a red-haired lassie can be found on either side of Loch Awe.' In 1510 she married Sir John Campbell, third son of the 2nd Earl of Argyll; and from them are descended in a direct line the Campbells of Calder, created Baron Cawdor in 1796 and Earl Cawdor of Castlemartin in 1827.

An enduring legend persists that a Thane of Cawdor (Calder) once dreamed that he should load a donkey with gold, let it loose, follow it, and build a great house wherever it came to rest. It slept for the night beneath a hawthorn tree, and to this day a tree can be seen in a vaulted basement beneath the main tower of Cawdor Castle. It has been radiocarbon-dated back to 1372, it is dead, and it is not a hawthorn but a holly tree. In mythology the holly (*Ilex aquifolium*) is one of seven sacred trees found in a Celtic grove.

Shakespeare's *Macbeth* (the 'Scottish play', as all actors call it, to avoid bad luck) is historically inaccurate in many respects. For a start he was a Thane of Glamis, not Cawdor. I now quote the late sixth Earl of Cawdor: 'The truth is that as Cawdor Castle was not built until the late fourteenth century, it is impossible for King Duncan to have lost any blood or Lady Macbeth much sleep in this particular house.'

The last British monarch to be born in Scotland was Charles I (1600–49), the second son of James VI of Scotland and of Anne of Denmark, who was created the Duke of Albany in the year of his birth in **Dunfermline Palace**, next to the **Abbey**. Andrew Carnegie (1835–1919), the great philanthropist who was also born in Dunfermline and made his fortune in America, presented Pittencrieff Park to the town in 1903, and within it stands the ruins of Malcolm's Tower. It was there that Dunfermline's very long connection with Scottish royalty commenced – with the marriage (his second) in *c.*1069 of Malcolm III (Canmore; *c.*1031–93) to the Saxon princess St Margaret (who was probably born in Hungary while her father Edward was in exile). They were to have six sons, Edward, Ethelred, Edmund, Edgar, Alexander I and David I, most of them buried on the Abbey site, and two daughters, one of whom, 'the Good Queen Maud', was born there and married Henry I of England.

The Abbey was founded as the Church of the Holy Trinity in 1072. David I, one of those sons, founded the Abbey in the first year of his reign (1124) with an abbot and 12 Benedictine monks brought north from Canterbury.

Cawdor Castle, where Lady Cawdor believes a monk is buried four and a half yards north-east of the tree shown on the right.

The dead holly tree in the vaulted basement of Cawdor Castle and reputed to be the reason for the location of the castle.

Malcolm III's body was moved there from Tynemouth in 1250, and most of his wife Margaret is also there. Her head went on its travels: Mary, Queen of Scots had it taken to Edinburgh Castle in 1560, and subsequently it was removed to the Laird of Durie's house in 1567; on it went, to the private keeping of some Jesuits in 1567, to Antwerp in 1620, and to the Scots College in Douai in 1627. Margaret's head finally vanished during the French Revolution.

Other Scottish monarchs buried in Dunfermline Abbey include Donald III (Bane; *c*.1031–1100), Edgar (*c*.1074–1107), Alexander I, 'the Fierce' (*c*.1077–1124) and his queen Sibylla (illegitimate daughter of Henry I of England), David I (*c*.1084–1153) and both his queens, Malcolm IV, 'the Maiden' (1141–1165), Alexander III (1241–1286), who fell over the cliff on his horse at Kinghorn, and, of course, King Robert the Bruce (1274–1329). Those last four words are spelt out in capital letters four feet high around the top of the abbey's 103-foot-high tower.

His body is not complete either. After his death 'the

Good Sir James' Douglas took his embalmed heart to Spain to join in the fight in the Crusades. Douglas was killed on 25 August 1330, and the heart was brought back to Scotland. It did not however join the rest of him, and was interred with great ceremony at Melrose Abbey, where its location was discovered in 1996.

Dunrobin Castle is the most northerly of Scotland's great houses, and one of the oldest which has been continuously inhabited. This seat of the Sutherlands is on a magnificent site overlooking the Dornoch Firth, north of Golspie. After his marriage in 1785 to Elizabeth, the Countess of Sutherland in her own right, the second Marquess of Stafford (later the first Duke of Sutherland; 1758–1833) initiated the so-called Sutherland Clearances in which more than 5,000 people were forcibly removed from their homes. Not a happy time. The estate grew until the third Duke (1828–1892) owned about 1,300,000 acres in Sutherland, making him western Europe's biggest landowner.

The castle has since been a naval hospital and a boys'

school, but now it is again the home of the family. One fact which has not changed over the centuries is the existence of Dunrobin Castle's two resident ghosts who occupy the top of the tower. In the fifteenth century, a wicked Earl of Sutherland locked up a beautiful young girl from the Mackay clan. She refused to marry him and tried to escape down sheets she had roped together. Furious, he cut the rope with his sword and she fell to her death. Today she is heard crying but is never seen. On the floor below, another (male) ghost is both seen and heard, but there is no tale of it. So there is a ghost with no story and a story with no ghost . . .

Dunure Castle, north-west of Maybole in Ayrshire, was the probable scene of a human roasting. Gilbert, fourth Earl of Cassillis (1517–1558), captured Allan Stewart, Commandator of nearby Crossraguel Abbey, put him in the vault, took off his clothes, bound him to a spit before a roaring fire, and commenced to roast him, not forgetting to baste the man with oil, like any efficient cook. He did all this because he wanted the abbey and its estate; don't ask, don't get.

Stewart, in the heat of the moment, signed away the property – but a few days later refused to go through with the deal. So Cassillis put him back on the spit for another session of roasting. Allan Stewart then gave him the signatures he wanted, put his clothes back on to his oily body and went off for a bath.

Many are the tales from **Dunvegan Castle** on the north-west side of the Isle of Skye. It is the seat of John MacLeod of MacLeod, who told me that when he came of age he was presented by his elder (yes, elder, but that is another story for another time) brother with Rory More's horn filled with nearly half a gallon of decent claret, which he consumed before his family on 14 August 1956 in one minute and 57 seconds, at one draught. 'Many rehearsals were needed,' he happily confided.

The Braham Seer predicted that if the famous Fairy Flag, which is preserved in the castle, is unfurled at a time of trouble for a third time then the clan MacLeod would lose their estate. The frail silk flag, of Near East origin and possibly brought back from a battle with Crusaders, has been produced twice: at Glendale, south-west of Dunvegan, in 1490, and at nearby Trumpan in 1580. The final use would have to be for some tremendous purpose.

There is a wicked Bottle Dungeon in the castle (reached from the second floor), the aspect of which is about as cheerful as the Bottle Dungeon in St Andrews Castle. The large fifteenth-century tower was added by Alasdair Crotach 'Crookback Alexander' MacLeod,

who must have had a thing about towers. Towards the end of his long life he actually lived in one at Rodel in the south of Harris (as mentioned in chapter two).

Fyvie Castle, a few miles south-east of Turriff, possesses a notebook-filling array of attractions to suit every imagination. Not far from the Hanging Tree observe the huge, bold and beautiful south front, with its finials in the form of musicians, the sculptured dormers, turrets, bartizans and crow-stepped gables. Not one but five towers here. The present thirteenth-century (when started) castle is on the site of an earlier one, and has passed through the hands of Edward I, Robert I, Robert III, Richard III, the Lindsays, Prestons, Meldrums, Setons, the English crown again, the Earls of Aberdeen, the Gordons and finally the Forbes-Leiths. It is now in the generous and sensitive care of The National Trust for Scotland.

The ghost of a Green Lady at Fyvie Castle has been mentioned in the previous chapter. A more tangible mystery is the Sealed Room, beneath the Charter Room. From the exterior you can spot on a wall a stone Turkish figure (apparently connected with Lord Byron), and below it there is a blocked-up slit window, and no other. Whoever breaks into the Sealed Room will die, and their husband or wife will go blind.

In the Douglas Room (also known as the 'Murder Room') hangs a portrait alleged to be of Margaret Hay, Countess of Dunfermline and wife of the first Earl (a Seton), painted in 1612 by an unknown hand. But is it in fact of a man? Perhaps it is really Henry, Prince of Wales (as he became in 1610), eldest son of James VI, who died of typhoid in the year it was painted . . .

Fyvie Castle possesses the finest wheel stair in Scotland. It is 18 feet in diameter and goes up three huge floors, its central newel post is not hollow (unlike the one at Glamis) and it is anticlockwise, for right-handed defenders descending, swords in hand. The pits on the stairs were caused by drunken Gordons riding their horses up them.

Late in the fourteenth century Sir Henry Preston had a visitor at a time when what is now called the Preston Tower was under construction and making use of stone from a local monastery. Thomas the Rymer, seer and poet, was not, to his surprise and then anger, offered traditional hospitality. When he heard that three stones of good shape had that very day been lost in the River Ythan, he issued a prediction – that until the three stones were re-united, Fyvie Castle would never pass down through more than two generations of the same family.

This has happened. One stone is somewhere in the

river; another is anonymously part of the stonework of the Preston Tower, and the third, now known as 'The Weeping Stone', can today be seen beneath a perspex case in the Lady's Chamber, partially decomposed. It is never dry, and is presumed to weep in its loneliness.

There is a splendid and rare earth closet, a thunder box (thanks to Evelyn Waugh), in a little wooden building in the grounds of Fyvie. You sat down on it, with sand lying beneath. When you finished, you piled earth on top like an animal, tugged at a pulley and away everything went, down a chute by the force of gravity and everything else. Servants removed the mixture each day.

The closet stands conveniently near an unusual construction, which the castle's last private family owners had put up in 1903. Sir Alexander Forbes-Leith, who bought the castle in 1889 (and was to become Lord Fyvie), made his fortune in American steel, and mixed with the Rockefellers, the Vanderbilts and other hard men of vision. He brought back to Scotland the new American rich man's toy: a playhouse. We would call it a private leisure centre today. He made a squash court, with a sliding wall so that it could be used as a hall for informal gatherings, and a ten-pin bowling alley complete with great big wooden balls with only two finger-holes in them.

Forbes-Leith also discovered the art of Tiffany in the States, which is why the Presbyterian Church in Fyvie village is the only church in Scotland with Tiffany glass in a window. It is dedicated to his youngest son, Percy Forbes Forbes-Leith, who died on active service in Natal on the last day of 1900.

Glamis Castle, south-west of Forfar, attracts great numbers of visitors for lots of good reasons. It belongs in the Queen Mother's family, being the seat of the Earls of Strathmore, it was her childhood home, and Princess Margaret was born there on 21 August 1930. Margaret Rose was the first royal scion in direct line of succession to the throne to be born in Scotland for three centuries.

There are those who say that the castle is the most haunted in the country – in spite of its romantic external appearance, with pointed turrets wherever you look – and that the hugely thick walls conceal a secret chamber, the entrance to which must only be known by three people or fewer. Perhaps it was there that a massively strong and grotesquely deformed member of the Strathmore family was hidden away some 200 years ago and did not die until the 1920s?

Stories persist of the ghost of the Grey Lady, seen near the chapel, who might or might not be the wife of the sixth Lord Glamis; James V had her burnt as a witch. And then there is Scotland's only black ghost – reputedly that of a negro servant who was very badly treated more than 200 years ago and is now very occasionally seen in the Queen Mother's sitting room.

Once upon a time there was a Ruthven Castle, just north-west of Perth, and it was built in the fifteenth century by the family of that name. Actually it is still standing, in the care of Historic Scotland, but now it is called **Huntingtower Castle**. The name change came about like this.

The 'Ruthven Raid' in 1582 is remembered for the capture of 16-year-old James VI (1566–1625). He was detained in the castle for ten long months, and planned his revenge. On 4 May 1585, by then free, he ordered that the head of the Earl of Gowrie (as the fourth Lord Ruthven had become) be separated from his body. The succeeding Earl and his brother were murdered in 1600, and then the King decreed, as only kings can, that the family name of Ruthven could no longer be used. Thus the castle was renamed.

The key gloss on this piece of history is that the young king was the son of Mary, Queen of Scots and Lord Darnley, and the third Lord Ruthven ('Patrick the Grim') had taken a leading part in the murder of David Rizzio (or Riccio), a particular favourite of Mary, Queen of Scots, at the Palace of Holyrood on 9 March 1566.

Now, back to the 'Ruthven Raid'. On the evening of the day it took place, the Earl's youngest daughter, Dorothea, was in bed with a secret lover. Not wishing to be caught and compromised, she made her escape by leaping across the 10-foot gap between the two square fortified towers. In the morning the two eloped.

It takes about seven minutes on the ferry from the Port of Menteith, four miles east of Aberfoyle, across the Lake (*not*, uniquely, Loch) of Menteith, to reach **Inchmahome Priory**. This Augustinian priory, on its magical island, was founded in 1238. In the surviving chapter house there is a touching sight, created in about 1290. It is a double tomb, in cold, eternal, dustless marble, and the representations of its occupants are facing each other, in an embrace. They are Walter Stewart, first Earl of Menteith, and his wife Mary.

Scone Palace, the seat of the Earls of Mansfield, a few miles north-east of Perth, is on the site of an old Augustinian abbey, founded in 1164 and demolished in 1559. It was built between 1803 and 1808 to a design

Fyvie Castle. Where the blocked slit window is, on the corner, there is a sealed, windowless room.

by William Atkinson — at a cost of £70,000. Atkinson put the present Music Gallery where he knew the abbey's former great hall was situated. This was where, as far back as the eighth century, coronations took place, because Old Scone (marked by a stone cross today) was the capital of Pictavia, one of the four kingdoms into which Scotland was then divided.

In the area around the palace (never a royal residence) there are two stone circles, a cairn, a Roman camp and road, and, most important of all, Mote or Moot Hill. This was a meeting place; there are high places with this name all over Britain. It is flat-topped, like all law hills, and it was first called *Tom-a-mhoid* — 'the hill where justice is administered'. In 710 it received a new name, christened, one might say, 'Castle of Belief' after Naitan, king of the Picts, announced that Easter and the resurrection would henceforth be observed. This led to the quarrel between Dalriadic Scots and the Picts which ultimately ended in a pact between them in 844 under Kenneth mac Alpin — and the beginning of Scotland as one nation.

The first Viscount Stormont built a parish church (now a ruin, but still with the Mansfield mausoleum within) on the flat top of the ancient law hill in about 1620, and it was there that the last coronation in Scotland took place — that of Charles II in 1651.

In 1402, a weird and mad human creature was carried, via a Welsh ship, to **Stirling Castle**, which had become a royal residence in 1371. The creature was known as 'The Mammet' — and was said to be Richard II of England (1367–1400), the younger son of Edward, the Black Prince. His supposed imposter fought and lost to the Duke of Hereford in August 1399, abdicated, was imprisoned (so most, though not all, history books confirm) in Pontefract, and apparently died a violent death there on 14 February 1400.

The King's personal chaplain occupies the tomb of Richard II in Westminster Abbey. The poor creature passed away in Stirling Castle in 1419 — and an English king now lies buried in Stirling; not in the castle, though, but beneath the road where Murray Place meets Station Road.

Stirling Castle, on its high, rocky promontory, positively drips with stories from the history of royalty

A typical Scottish doocot (dovecot) of elaborate design.

in Scotland. Here is just one, of a not very private occasion: a banquet in the Parliament House after the baptism, in a newly built chapel on 30 August 1594, of Prince Henry, eldest son of James VI (he who may be portrayed in the strange portrait in Fyvie Castle). This is an old account of the occasion:

The kings, queens and ambassadors were all placed at one table, being formed in three parts, in a geometrical figure, so that everyone might have a full sight of the other.

During the progress of the feast a triumphal car, seemingly drawn by a Moorish slave, entered, full of delicacies, which were distributed among the guests by six damsels clothed in satin and glittering with gold and silver. Thereafter there entered a boat 18 feet in length, placed upon wheels and moved by invisible springs. The masts which were 40 feet high, were red, the ropes of red silk, and the blocks were of gold. The sails were of white taffeta, and the anchors were tipped with silver. She was loaded with sweetmeats, and on board were Neptune, Thetis, Arion and Triton, while three sirens floated in the artificial sea that surrounded the vessel.

On an islet in the River Dee in Kirkcudbrightshire looms **Threave Castle**. It was built by Archibald 'the Grim', third Earl of Douglas (the natural son of 'The Good Sir James'; *c.*1330–1400), of the 'Black Douglases', at the end of the fourteenth century. It is ten minutes' walk from the car park in Balmaghie, and then you ring the bell for the ferry to the roofless ruins.

William, eighth Earl of Douglas (*c.*1425–*c.*1452), was a very nasty piece of work, and married his cousin ('The Maid of Galloway'). At the end of his life he maintained a force of over 1,000 men in the castle, and formed the notion that he wanted to acquire the head of Sir Patrick MacLellan, a neighbour. He bribed a servant to betray the laird, which he duly did. The servant then arrived to claim the spoonful of gold he had been promised, and he received it . . . down his throat.

James, ninth Earl of Douglas (1426–1488), was the brother of the eighth Earl and married his widow. He went on to lose Threave Castle in 1455 to royalist forces, who possessed one mighty weapon of war,

Dunvegan Castle overlooking Loch Dunvegan in the north-west of Skye. As the flag is flying, the Chief MacLeod of MacLeod must be in residence.

known as 'Mons Meg'. It was a cannon nearly 14 feet long, with a bore of nearly two feet. The castle was finally ruined by the Covenanters in 1640, and left as we see it today.

The poet John Gay put it well: 'Envy is a kind of praise.' I envy the 21st Lady of Traquair, Catherine Maxwell Stuart, because she and her mother are in possession of one of Scotland's most wonderful homes, **Traquair House**, south of Innerleithen, and I praise her because it is open to the public and, quite as important, she actively encourages the pursuit of arts and crafts on the estate.

In chapter seven, in connection with the Traquair House ale, I told the story of the Bear Gates and their permanent closure in 1795 by the fifth Earl of Traquair (1697–1764). There is another version of that story, which says that the gates shall not be reopened until once again there is a Countess of Traquair. Well, there was one subsequently because the seventh and penultimate Earl, Charles Stuart (1746–1827), married Mary Ravenscroft of Wickham in 1773.

The house witnessed a positive wave of fecundity between 1697 and 1711. Charles, fourth Earl of Traquair (and the tenth Laird), a Jacobite involved in the 1715 rising, and his wife Lady Mary Maxwell, only daughter of the fourth Earl of Nithsdale, produced 17 children (including two sets of twins), all of whom survived. Traquair House is one of Scotland's oldest homes to be occupied continuously by one family, and with that kind of track record in the family its future looks assured, whether or not the Bear Gates are reopened. And there is character in the family blood as well. The first Earl of Traquair, John Stuart (1600–1659), once decided he wanted to fish for salmon from his bedroom window – so he had a tributary of the River Tweed especially created.

Chapter Eleven

TARTAN TALES, AND ALL THAT

There is a glorious confusion about the Scottish tartans. The word derives from the French *tartaine* or (variously) *tiretane*, meaning simply a kind of material. It was not from the Gaelic *breacan*, multi-coloured or striped cloth. Nor has a tartan pattern, or sett, always been associated with a particular clan or family name.

In the 1538 Exchequer Rolls of King James V's Lord High Treasurer a cloth bale of '*Heland Tartane*' is accounted for; but *Heland* could have referred to a cut for the King's trews and not to the Highlands, for the bale was intended for the '*hoiss*' (stocking hose) '*to the Kingis Grace*'. The Gaelic *breacan*, now tartan plaid, was in some sixteenth- and early seventeenth-century accounts, attached to the Old Irish *brat* (mantle), producing *breachbrait*, and engravings from the later period depict a tartan mantle as part of a Black Watch regimental uniform. This great regiment was formed in 1729, and the Campbells soon claimed this tartan as their own. And so it has remained.

The Campbells, of Argyll, Breadalbane, Cawdor and London, were one of the first clans to 'acquire' a tartan for themselves, but Martin Martin had noted in the 1690s that in the Hebrides, individual setts of tartan plaid were permanently adopted by the islanders, with their patterns recorded on sett sticks.

These sticks were to become important. After the 1745 Jacobite uprising, the *Breacan Vallach* (Gallant Tartan) kilt, and all other forms of Highland dress, were banned by the English (until 1782), except for legally formed units of soldiers. The Highland Society of London started its collection of tartans in 1816 and fanned into life a truly national enthusiasm for tartan setts, with the ardent support of Queen Victoria and Sir Walter Scott.

There is still no official body to regulate the design and manufacture of tartans. In theory, we all have the 'right' to wear any tartan we may choose. But I for one would never test such a theory in certain locations. I know of chiefs who would soon be having a not-so-quiet word with me, within large, cold cellars.

The earliest tartans depended for their colours on local sources of colour dye. The ubiquitous green came from mosses, and excellent colorants were provided by certain plants, such as bilberry, birch, bird's foot trefoil, blackthorn, bog myrtle, bramble, crowberry, devil's bit scabious, elderberry, heather, ladies' bedstraw, St John's wort, sundew, yellow iris and water-lily. The last produces black.

Wool colours need 'fixing' – and available, convenient agents have long been sought out for this process – for example, alum, copper, fir-club moss and iron. Freshly spun Harris Tweed can give off the smell of another freely available and very convenient fixing agent called urine. Harris Tweed is actually made on Lewis. The sound of shuttles can always be heard around Lewis, as surely as the smell from the year-round spirals of peat smoke can be detected rising from beside the front-room looms.

The surname Fleming is commonly found in the Borders because 400 and more years ago Flemish weavers worked in the great Border abbeys with their co-patriot monks from Flanders. *Pleat* is one Gaelic verb for 'weave'. Woven cloth went off for finishing at 'waulk-mills' at places like Hawick, Melrose and Selkirk.

The Scottish Tartans Society has on record some 250 different tartan designs. Each of them employs a basic piece of algebra. The total number of shades is calculated by applying the formula $(x + 1)\,{}^{x}/_{2}$ where x represents the number of colours he has available for his dyes. Three colours therefore give (4×3) divided by 2, which is six shades. Four colours give ten shades etc.

Some Scottish wool products have long been famed, and odd stories are attached to them – cheviot cloth, for example. The lofty Cheviot hills range for 25 miles along the Borders; their hardy, large-bodied sheep were brought up north to Caithness in 1792 by a remarkable man. Sir John Sinclair, Bt., was a true polymath: MP for Caithness for 31 years, possessor (as his statue in St John's Square Gardens, Thurso, states) of diplomas from 13 foreign countries and the author of 367 publications. When he retired, 22 Scottish counties voted thanks to him for his services; his statue plaque states that about 200 persons owed their success in life to him. Sir John expressed all through his life that a real Scotsman should prefer tartan trews to a kilt. And he introduced organised sheep-shearing to help the habit along.

In St John's Square itself stands a statue of his father, Sir George Sinclair, who also lived in the family seat of Thurso Castle. The inscription below confirms for us that between 1845 and 1852 he did not spend a single night away from home. Is it him or his wife we should admire?

The kilts that Sir John Sinclair abhorred are generally regarded now as part of the formal Scottish national uniform. The lore and legends of what, if anything, is worn beneath them, are best left where they came from. But there is no doubting today that the chief of a clan in the kilt sett of his inheritance can be a fine sight.

The Act of Union with England in 1707 united Scotland against England on a national scale for the first time. Lowlanders saw the power and virtues of the clan system in the north and took up more widely many of its traditions. One was the common wearing of kilts of a particular sett within certain national geographical enclaves and among prominent families. Habits from the Highlands were being adopted.

The word 'clan' comes down to us from the Latin word *planta*, meaning 'sprout'. The Gaels of Ireland and the Highlands substituted the 'k' for the 'p'; it then evolved into *clann*, preserving its sense of a group of people claiming common ancestry and remaining associated in common causes. A tribe of sprogs, as one might put it. But this in no way means, should your surname be, for example, Mackintosh, that you automatically have membership of the *clann an Toisich* — the clan Mackintosh (*Mac* means 'son'). For that you would need to contact the Clan Secretary, and do bear in mind the clan's motto 'Touch not the cat bot a glove'. However, it may be that you are indeed a kinsman of Charles Mackintosh (1766–1843), inventor of the waterproof coat, and Charles Rennie Mackintosh (1868–1928), architect, designer and painter.

Bagpipes were in full use by the end of the sixteenth century, generally replacing the Scottish harp (the *clàrsach*), a gentle instrument. The bagpipe was not *chó caoin ri clàrsach* (as melodious as the harp), but much more an instrument of celebration, war and lament. But its origins may be centuries earlier, because a depiction of one is carved in stone in Rosslyn Chapel (known for its fabulous and profuse carvings), between Penicuik and Lasswade in Midlothian.

The first pibroch, the finest bagpipe musical form, was composed in 1603 by Donald Mor MacCrimmon of a family who were to become hereditary pipers to the MacLeods of Dunvegan on Skye. The MacCrimmon college of piping at Boreraig on the island existed through six generations.

The dance tunes of strathspeys and reels played on fiddles are best known at *ceilidhs* — literally 'visits' but now meaning musical gatherings. At these there are constantly recalled Gaelic songs, many centuries old. The destruction of the old Gael way of life and the Highland Clearances meant that thousands of stories and songs are gone for ever. Collections of those not lost have been made along the way, however, and recent years have seen an exciting revival of general interest in all matters Gaelic.

The first musical sounds made in Scotland were probably created on rocks that gave out ringing sounds or musical echoes when they were struck hard. The oldest playable musical instrument in Scotland is a bronze horn from about 300 BC, which resides in Caprington Castle, south-west of Kilmarnock.

It has been claimed that Old Coel the Splendid (or Coelus), a king in Ayrshire at the end of the Roman period, inspired the nursery rhyme 'Old King Cole'. This gentleman is reputed to be buried in a mound in the grounds of Coilsfield House, in Coylton, five miles south-east of Ayr. This circular mound, or tumulus, was opened in 1837 and found to contain four cinerary urns.

When you next sing 'O Come All Ye Faithful', remember that it was probably written by John Wade Francis, as a coded rallying cry to all Jacobites. It was first heard just before the 1745 uprising.

Scots believe that if they die when they are abroad, their souls return to the land of their birth through underground passages, with caves as resting places along the way. This is the 'low road' mentioned in the famous song 'The Bonnie Banks o' Loch Lomon''. It is held that the song is in fact a conversation between two prisoners, one of whom is due to be executed; the other will soon be free to return by the high road, which is to say an ordinary road.

Nowadays, the term 'controversialist' is not often used in print, but it exactly describes Halliday Gibson Sutherland (1882–1960), whom I have quoted earlier. He was also a physician, worked on tuberculosis in London, served in the Navy and the Air Force

This extract, in spoken Scots, from Robert Louis Stevenson's short story *Thrawn Janet*, incorporates the common ancient belief that the Devil appears as a black man. Recorded trials of witches bear similar testimony.

Abune Hangin' Shaw, in the bield o' the Black Hill, there's a bit enclosed grund wi' an iron yett; and it seems, in the auld days, that was the kirkyaird o' Ba'weary, and consecrated by the Papists before the blessed licht shone upon the kingdom. It was a great howff o' Mr. Soulis's, onyway; there he would sit an' consider his sermons; and indeed it's a bieldy bit. Weel, as he cam' ower the wast end o' the Black Hill, ae day, he saw first twa, an syne fower, an' syne seeven corbie craws fleein' round an' round abune the auld kirkyaird. They flew laigh and heavy, an' squawked to ither as they gaed; and it was clear to Mr. Soulis that something had put them frae their ordinar. He wasnae easy fleyed, an' what suld he find there but a man, or the appearance of a man, sittin' in the inside upon a grave. He was of great stature, an' black as hell, and his e'en were singular to see. Mr. Soulis had heard tell o' black men, mony's the time; but there was something unco about this black man that daunted him. Het as he was, he took a kind o' cauld grue in the marrow o' his banes . . . That was a nicht that has never been forgotten in Ba'weary. The nicht o' the seventeenth of August, seventeen hun'er' an' twal'.

during the First World War, contested Marie Stopes's views on birth control, won a libel action against her and also a wrote a best-selling volume of biography called *Arches of the Years* in 1933. In the chapter entitled 'Arcadia' he wrote as follows:

In the woods were fairies. They were mostly neutral beings who did not hurt you unless you hurt them. If you did offend them they could be vindictive. They would take a baby out of its cot and put a changeling in its place. Mr. Cameron had once seen a fairy funeral crossing the road from one wood to another. There was the little hearse, about a foot high, drawn by four little horses, and followed by a long procession of the little people. His friend, Angus Macdonald, had once

seen the same thing, and had thought it was all his imagination. He drove his horse and cart through the procession, and, as he passed over it, the procession faded from the road, although he could still see the little people in the wood on either side. When he reached home his wife said to him: 'That stairway is very narrow. I couldna' get the arm-chair out of the kitchen up to the bedroom.' A week later he was dead, and his coffin had to be taken out of the window because the stairs were too narrow.

Then there was Donald Grant's boy, aged eight. He found a cheese in the woods and brought it home. 'Take it back where ye got it,' said his father. 'It's a fairy cheese.' The boy took the cheese away, but hid it in an outhouse, where he ate it in secret. In the hayfield a

This gate in north-west Lewis confirms an old belief among farmers that it is unlucky to remove one, even if the attached wall or fence has had to go. The Biblical connotation of a gateway is an unblocked path.

week later he fell on the scythe, cut the main artery in his thigh and bled to death in a few minutes.

Some fairies are capricious, and that is why you never name another person when walking in the woods at night. The fairies might overhear the name, and, once they knew it, could entice the person away. Fairies also dislike to hear humans boasting, so you never said: 'That's a fine field of corn,' but always, 'That corn is no' so bad,' because they have power to put a blight on crops. There was only one way in which crops could be protected: if a virgin walked naked round the fields at midnight, but none must see her walk.

Ancient beliefs and centuries-old traditions, particularly in the Highlands and islands, have their resonance in many occasions and ceremonies which we still enjoy today. These passages give a distinct flavour of 'how things were done'.

Halliday Sutherland described 'bundling' on Lewis:

Amongst the people of the black houses, there is a

curious custom in courtship and, like all primitive sex customs, it is based on economic conditions. The time for making love is during the long winter nights when the young men are at home. On that bleak windswept coast it would be difficult for two people to make love out of doors so the young man goes to the girl's house. Again with one living room where the family are living it is difficult to make love. The girl goes into the sleeping room. There is no fire there, nor any light, because the burning of tallow candles and oil is a consideration to people who are poor. So, for warmth, the girl goes to bed. Once in bed, both her legs are inserted into one large stocking, which her mother ties above her knees. Then the young man goes into the sleeping room, and lies beside her.

If Halliday Sutherland's couple survived this routine in one of the smoky black houses and proceeded to marriage, and if that in time proved not to work out satisfactorily, they could have repaired to the Chapel of

146

Biblical admonitions above a restaurant on the corner of High Street and Church Street, opposite the Town Hall in Inverness.

St Coivan, which is between Campbeltown and Machrihanish in the south of Kintyre. On a particular midnight each year all couples who were unhappy with their marriages were blindfolded and asked to proceed around the church. When St Coivan called out *greimich* ('seize'), every man had to catch hold of a woman. That woman was to remain his wife for the next 12 months at least.

However, the tradition of 'handfasting' was both ancient and popular. A couple could live together, with or without their parents' permission, until they decided whether they would marry or not. They had 12 months in which to decide whether their handfasting was to proceed to formal marriage. If they did decide to marry, the marriage ceremony took place one year and one day after they first handfasted. If any children were born of that temporary union the child became the responsibility of the father and, strangely, the reputation of the mother was never questioned. Martin Martin recorded that this custom died out in the early sixteenth century.

Marriages that lasted were well undertaken. Here a priest, Walter Gregor, writes of them in 1874:

Early marriage rules among the fishing population. Their occupation calls for this. Much of its work, such as the gathering of the bait, the preparing of it, the baiting of the fishing lines, the cleaning and curing of the fish, and the selling of them, is done by women.

The mode of bringing about and arranging the marriage is not uniform. Here is one mode. When a young man wishes to marry, his father is told. The father goes to the parents of the young maiden on whom his son has fixed his fancy, gives a detail of what he is worth as to his worldly gear, and recounts all his good qualities. If the offer is accepted, a nicht is fixed when the two meet along with their friends, and the final arrangement is made. This meeting goes by the name of the *beukin nicht*, or the *nicht o' the greeance*.

Of an evening shortly before the marriage day, or on the evening before the marriage, the bride and bridegroom set out in company often hand in hand to

147

The burial ground of the Clan Macnab, near Kinnell.

A very jolly letterbox for 5A McLeod, on the road from Stornoway to Callanish on Lewis.

invite the guests. The bridegroom carries a piece of chalk, and, if he finds the door of any of his friends' houses shut, he makes a cross on it with his chalk. This mark is understood as an invitation to the marriage. A common form of words in giving the invitation is: 'Ye ken faht's adee the morn at twal o'clock. Come our in fess a' yir oose wi ye', or, 'Come ane, come athegeethir'. The number of guests is usually large, ranging from forty to a hundred or a hundred and twenty.

In one, if not more, of the villages, when the marriage takes place at the home of the bride, after the rite is concluded the whole of the marriage party makes the circuit of the village. The bride is married in full travelling attire, and all the women present are in the same costume. Special notice is taken of the *first fit*, and the success of the future life is divined from it. A man with a white horse is deemed most propitious.

When a sailor is married, immediately on the conclusion of the rite the two youngest sailor-apprentices in the harbour at the time march into the room carrying the Union Jack. The bride is completely wrapped in it along with the youngest

apprentice, who has the privilege of kissing her.

When the bride is entering her future home, two of her female friends meet her at the door, the one bearing a towel or napkin, and the other a dish filled with various kinds of bread. The towel or napkin is spread over her head, and the bread is then poured over her. It is gathered up by the children who have collected round the door. In former times the bride was then led up to the hearth, and, after the fire had been scattered, the tongs was put into her hand and she made it up.

It is usual, at least among the well-to-do fishermen, for the bride to bring to her new home a chest of drawers, a *kist*, a feather bed, four pairs of white blankets, two bolsters, four pillows, sheets, one dozen towels, a table-cloth, all the hardware, cogs, tubs, and a *sheelin coug*.

The young maiden begins commonly at an early age to collect feathers for her bed and pillows, and her admirers or her affianced lends help by shooting wild-fowl for her. Out of her first earnings is bought a *kist*, and she goes on adding one thing to another till her

This Highland croft, near Dornoch, survived the dreaded Clearances.

providan is complete. The husband's part is to provide the chairs, tables etc., and all the fishing gear.

It was an old Scottish tradition that the ceremony of marriage is best avoided in the month of May, because the bride then may not be too good at handling money. Another one, noted in the Shetland Islands in the mid-nineteenth century, is that a successful marriage must take place on a day when a new moon is due. The best man slept with the bride-to-be on the eve of her wedding, but left before breakfast for a prenuptial feast with the groom. Following that, the groom and his backers or ushers walked to the bride's dwelling, where three shots were fired into the air. After the third, the bride's door was opened and she would lead her 15 or so bridesmaids out and walk clockwise, following the sun, right around him. Scottish reels so often reflect this wheeling motion.

Such details are from an account by Robert Jamieson published in Edinburgh in 1869. He continued thus, and the detailed traditions of this wedding celebration would be wonderful to duplicate today.

On the conclusion of the ceremony, which is generally performed in the manse kitchen, the 'honest man' goes round with a bottle of wine or brandy, offering each of the company a glass, and the 'honest woman' follows with a basket of biscuit or cake. There is always a 'gunner' in every company and on returning from the manse, shots are fired as fast as the gun can be loaded, while with every shot there issues from the throat of each man a vociferous 'hip-hip-hurrah'. As they approach the bride's house, her mother and one or two female relatives meet her, carrying in a clean white cambric napkin a cake baked with seeds and sugar, called the 'bride's-cake' or 'dreaming-bread', broken into small pieces, which she throws over the head of the bride.

Dinner is now on the table – a dinner, I believe, peculiar to Shetland weddings. The fire has been removed from the centre of the floor, and the table, formed of chests, extends the whole length of the house, and is covered with white cotton. The dinner consists of a savoury dish of 'stove' made of five or six fat newly-slaughtered sheep, cut into small pieces with

149

This sign, by Golspie High School in Sutherland, challenges the imagination.

an axe, and boiled in the largest 'kettle' in the neighbourhood: it is seasoned with salt, pepper and caraway seeds, and served boiling hot in huge dishes, around each of which are laid a number of cow's-horn spoons. The company are seated each opposite his own partner; grace is said; and fortunate is he who has secured a spoon with a long handle, since in a few minutes the short-handled ones become encased in a mass of mutton-fat. Oatcakes are eaten along with the 'stove', and a glass of whisky concludes the repast.

Tea, or the 'bride's piece', is generally over about six o'clock; the floor is cleared, the fiddler is elevated on the top of a chest, and dancing commences. About nine o'clock, commotion and whispering being observed among those nearest the door, the fiddler stops, dancing ceases, and the 'honest man' informs the company that the 'guisers' have arrived. On the best man's announcing that there is plenty of both meat and drink for all comers — five gallons of whisky, it may be, yet untouched — the fiddler is told to 'play up the guisers' spring'.

In walks a tall, slender-looking man, called the 'scuddler', his face closely veiled with a white cambric

napkin, and on his head a cap made of straw, in shape like a sugar loaf, with three loops at the upper extremity, filled with ribbons of every conceivable hue, and hanging down so as nearly to cover the cap. He wears a white shirt, with a band of ribbons around each arm, and a bunch of ribbons on each shoulder, with a petticoat of long clean straw (called 'gloy') which hangs loosely. The moment he enters he gives a snore, and having danced for a few minutes, another enters, called the 'gentleman', somewhat similarly attired: he, too, having danced, a third, called the 'fool', appears, and so on till all are in. And it is really a strange sight to see six tall young men dressed thus fantastically, and dancing with so much earnestness. They are careful to speak not a word lest they reveal their identity; and not a sound is heard but the music of the fiddle, the rustle of the straw petticoats, the thud of their feet on the earthen floor, the laughter of the 'fool', and the whispers of the bride's maidens guessing who the guisers may be.

Dancing is kept up by the company till far on in the small hours, and supper is at last announced . . . a simple repast of sowans and milk, after which they

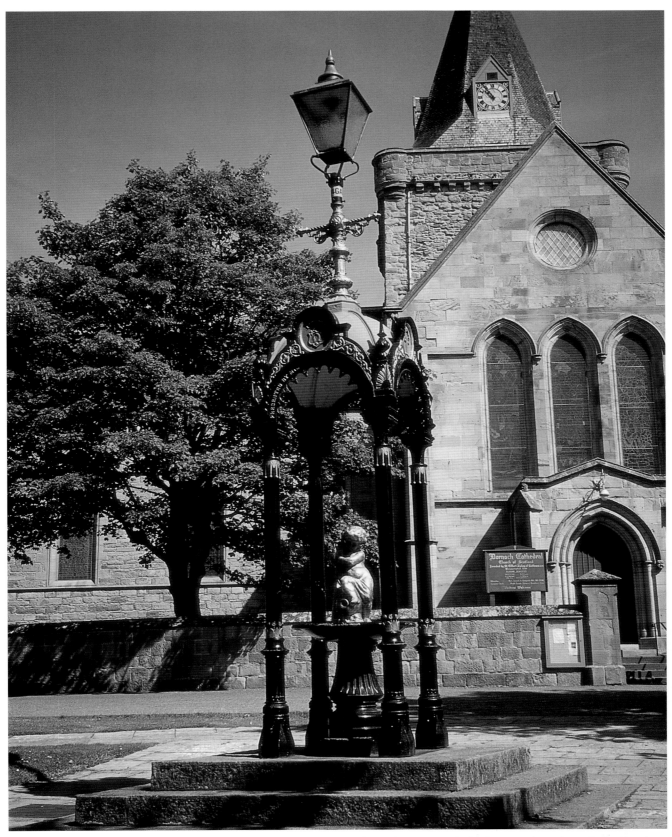

This fountain outside the Cathedral at Dornoch was erected by Miss Georgina Anderson (1821–1899), daughter of a fish merchant who became a sheep farmer. Notice the four shields on the canopy. On the north side, with the words Sans peur, *is the Sutherland crest. On the south, with a horseshoe and the words* Without feare, *is the crest of the Royal Burgh of Dornoch. On the west side, with the words* Dread God *and an eagle below, are the arms of the clan Munro (Miss Anderson's mother was a Munro), while the shield on the east side bears the Anderson arms . . . but what could the crocodiles represent?*

This house, on the A9 near Pitlochry, is believed to be the very centre of Scotland.

retire for the night. About ten am they reassemble, have breakfast, walk in procession for two or three hours, take dinner, and then finally separate.

In a book with the title *Mysterious Scotland*, loose ends are inevitable, as are sudden changes of theme. Here are two modern mysteries which, for all their tragedy, would find a place in a book such as this were it being written in a hundred years' time.

Two air crashes in recent years have occurred in Scotland and in neither case have the exact causes and perpetrators been identified. A PanAm Boeing 747 crashed on the evening of 21 December 1988 on to the town of Lockerbie in Dumfriesshire. It was Britain's largest air disaster; all 243 passengers and 16 crew were killed, as were many more on the ground. The presumption is that it was caused by a bomb on board which had been concealed in a transistor radio by two Libyans. The plane had broken up into five pieces the moment the bomb went off. There had previously been no mayday call from the pilot.

On 2 June 1994, the RAF's worst peacetime helicopter tragedy occurred on the Mull of Kintyre. An RAF Chinook Mark 2 helicopter HC2 ZD576 was flying from Belfast up towards Fort George, an army base near Inverness. On board were ten members of the RUC Special Branch, six MI5 officers, nine army intelligence officers and four crew members. They were going to attend a conference which could possibly have moved forward the peace process in Northern Ireland following the previous December's Downing Street Declaration.

There could not have been a more valuable collection of personnel gathered in one place, and it has been suggested that they should never have flown together. The government statement after the first court of inquiry reported that the pilots were guilty of negligence; however, this is held not to be so, and there certainly is a mystery that has extraordinary similarities with the circumstances in which the Duke of Kent lost his life up in the north-east (see chapter four).

The pilot's route map was very clearly marked. He was to leave Belfast, head over County Antrim, the Irish Sea, the Mull of Kintyre and the Scottish mainland, north to Fort George. He and his co-pilot were extremely experienced, as was the case in the Duke of Kent's plane. Amid heavy ground mists and swathes of fog and driving rain, the Chinook rammed into the side

Hamish is very much in charge, in the grounds of Cawdor Castle.

A tree sculpture by Frank Bruce of Banff. 'I looked at modern abstract sculpture and couldn't find a framework. So I took the abstractions already in the trees to carve my figures and say what I was trying to say!'

White horses have always been the subject of superstition. Kept among cattle, they bring good health to the stock.

Scotland's secret bunker at Troywood, near St Andrews in Fife, survives to remind us of the Cold War years after World War II ended. It was constructed far underground beneath a remote farmhouse (which has welcomed visitors since 1994) where, if necessary, Britain's central government and military commanders would have run the country if nuclear war had broken out. The main tunnel leading to a labyrinthine maze of concrete bunkers is 150 yards long. There was a permanent staff of 60, and it would have been possible to make international broadcasts from a studio there. It has 2,800 external telephone lines and 500 internal extensions. And until 1983 the public never knew it was there.

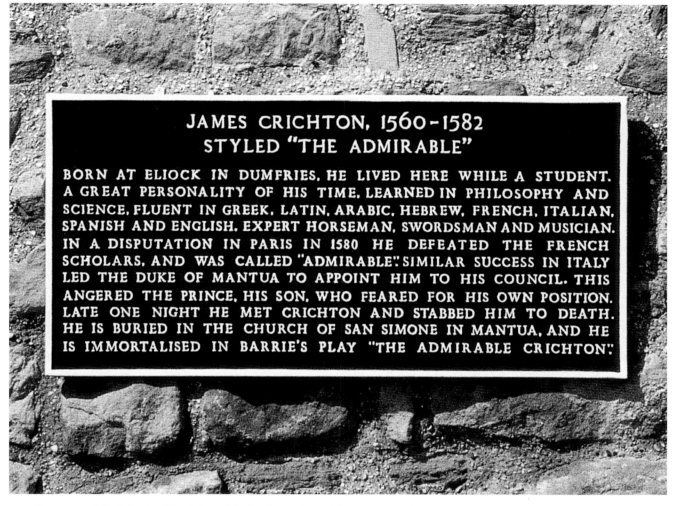

JAMES CRICHTON, 1560-1582
STYLED "THE ADMIRABLE"

BORN AT ELIOCK IN DUMFRIES, HE LIVED HERE WHILE A STUDENT. A GREAT PERSONALITY OF HIS TIME, LEARNED IN PHILOSOPHY AND SCIENCE, FLUENT IN GREEK, LATIN, ARABIC, HEBREW, FRENCH, ITALIAN, SPANISH AND ENGLISH, EXPERT HORSEMAN, SWORDSMAN AND MUSICIAN. IN A DISPUTATION IN PARIS IN 1580 HE DEFEATED THE FRENCH SCHOLARS, AND WAS CALLED "ADMIRABLE". SIMILAR SUCCESS IN ITALY LED THE DUKE OF MANTUA TO APPOINT HIM TO HIS COUNCIL. THIS ANGERED THE PRINCE, HIS SON, WHO FEARED FOR HIS OWN POSITION. LATE ONE NIGHT HE MET CRICHTON AND STABBED HIM TO DEATH. HE IS BURIED IN THE CHURCH OF SAN SIMONE IN MANTUA, AND HE IS IMMORTALISED IN BARRIE'S PLAY "THE ADMIRABLE CRICHTON".

The true story behind the play The Admirable Crichton *(1902) by J.M. Barrie (1860–1937), the ninth son of a Kirriemuir weaver. He was greatly affected all his life by the death of a brother when he was six years old.*

of a small cliff on the side of Torr Mor, a 1,400-foot hill in the south-west of the Mull. The helicopter should have been flying at a minimum of 2,800 feet, but it hit the hillside at 810 feet at over 100 miles an hour and climbing at 30°, which is called a cruise climb. There have of course been many theories about this disaster and how it happened.

Was it really pilot error, with the instruments misread and the pilot possibly dropping below the cloud base to get his bearings? Or was there engine failure, perhaps due to birds entering the blades? Was there instrument failure? Could the altimeter have been

affected in some unknown way? Or was there gear failure, which has occurred in previous RAF Chinook accidents? Subsequent investigations revealed that there was, unusually, no black box on board, and of course there were no survivors to comment as to why no mayday call was sent out. The first inquiry ruled out any mechanical failure, sabotage – or the rumoured use of mobile phones on board which could have affected instrumentation. And so a horrible mystery remains. A modern one, but unsolved, like so many in this book. Scotland keeps its secrets.

INDEX

Callanish, 'The Stonehenge of the North', on the Isle of Lewis.